− 7   639.395

R.D. Bartlett and Patricia P. Bartlett H97

Anoles, Basilisks, and Water Dragons

With 72 Color Photographs

Illustrations by Michele Earle-Bridges

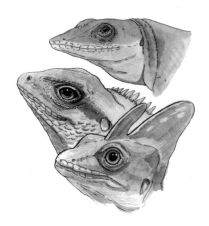

All inquiries should be addressed to:
 ̀rron's Educational Series, Inc.
250 Wireless Boulevard
Hauppauge, NY 11788

International Standard Book No. 0-7641-9789-0

Library of Congress Catalog Card No. 96-46980

Library of Congress Cataloging-in-Publication Data
Bartlett, Richard D., 1938–
     Anoles, basilisks, and water dragons : a complete pet
care manual / by R.D. Bartlett and Patricia Bartlett.
          p.   cm.
     Includes bibliographical references and index.
     ISBN 0-8120-9789-0
     1. Lizards as pets. I. Bartlett, Patricia Pope,
1949–   . II. Title.
SF459.L5B36   1997
639.3′95—dc21   96-46980
                                                   CIP

Printed in Hong Kong

9876543

About the Authors

R.D. Bartlett is a herpetologist who has authored more than 400 articles and three books, and coauthored an additional eight books. He lectures extensively and has participated in field studies across North and Latin America. He is a member of numerous herpetological and conservation organizations, a co-host on an "on-line" reptile and amphibian forum, and a contributing editor of *Reptiles Magazine*.

Patricia Bartlett is a biologist and historian who has authored five books and coauthored eight books. A museum administrator for the last fifteen years, she has worked in both history and science museums. In 1970 the Bartletts began the Reptilian Breeding and Research Institute, a private facility. Since its inception, more than 200 species of reptiles and amphibians have been bred at RBRI, some for the first time in the United States under captive conditions. Successes at the RBRI include several endangered species.

Acknowledgments

As there is in any compilation of notes and material, when this type of book is written, personal input from others in the field is sought. Such was the case here. Bill Love and Rob MacInnes of Glades Herp (Ft. Myers, Florida) called when unusual species became available and allowed unlimited photographic opportunities. Chris McQuade and Eric Thiss (Gulf Coast Reptiles, Ft. Myers, Florida) were equally generous. A trip with Bill Lamar (Green Tracks Ecotours) to Amazonian Peru yielded photos of several interesting anoles. Roger Kilhefner kindly advised us of populations of large-headed and Haitian green anoles in south Florida. Walt Meshaka helped locate the Florida strongholds of several other species of anoles and basilisks. In a manner most typical, both Ernie Wagner and Fredric L. Frye, DVM, offered thoughts and comments that enabled us to more quickly arrive at the finished product. To all of these and our editor, Amanda Pisani, our most sincere thanks.

Photo Credits

Zig Leszczynski: inside back cover, pages 36, 77, 84, 85 top; Bert Langerwerf: pages 33, 83 top left, 83 top right, 85 bottom; all other photographs by R.D. Bartlett.

Cover Photos

Front cover: Brown Anole, *Anolis sagrei* ssp.; inside front cover: Green Anole, *Anole carolinensis;* inside back cover: Green Water Dragon, *Physignathus cocincinus;* back cover: Green Basilisk, *Basiliscus plumifrons.*

Contents

Preface

It is not always necessary for a lizard to be rare or even uncommon to catch the fancy of reptile enthusiasts. Sometimes something other than rarity prevails. This "something" is threefold in the case of the little green anole, one of the most common lizards in the United States. Green anoles have the remarkable ability to change color and, because of their expanded and specialized toetips, they can walk straight up a vertical pane of glass. Because of their abundance, green anoles are so inexpensive that nearly anyone can purchase one. This set of characteristics almost assures that anyone who meets a green anole will want to know more.

A half-century ago, the green anole was about the only lizard species seen in the American pet trade. Today it is possible to find a hundred or more lizard species offered on a regular basis. These run the gamut from uncommon 8-foot-long (2.4 m) crocodile monitors to 3-inch-long (7.6 cm) house geckos that are anything but uncommon.

Green anoles are still offered in almost any store where lizards are sold, introducing one generation after another to the fascinating world of lizard husbandry—and the price today is hardly any different than it was 50 years ago.

What *has* changed are our husbandry techniques. The conventional wisdom of 50 years ago was that green anoles (then called American chameleons) would survive on a diet of sugar water, and that they could assume the color and pattern of their background, whatever that might have been. Some of us may remember placing an anole on a plaid surface and waiting patiently for the color change that of course never took place.

We now know that anoles (correctly pronounced *a-nole-ee*, by the way, but almost always pronounced *an-ole*) are primarily insectivorous and that the color changes (of those species capable of changing color) are stress related.

Many of the highly arboreal anoles, like our green, can assume a body color of bright green, but may, more often, be brown. Some, like the brown anole, a "Johnny-come-lately" species in the United States, may alter the shade of brown somewhat, but are never green. Species that are able to assume a green coloration are generally canopy species—lizards that are entirely at home high in the crown of lofty trees. The brown species, on the other hand, are often found amidst ground litter where they are almost perfectly camouflaged.

We became interested in anoles many years ago when the lizards were sold at fairs and sportsmen's shows. When, a few years later, we were asked if we'd like to see these little lizards in the field, we snapped up the chance. As years passed, we saw anoles of many kinds in Florida, Mexico, and several Central and South American countries. We watched them drinking from pendulous, jeweled droplets of afternoon rain and snatching up ants and tiny beetles on the trunks of palms. We saw them ghosting over motel windows, and heard them scurrying through dry leaves.

As time went on, "new" anole species escaped from the pet trade and colonized Florida. Thirty years ago, we saw our first knight anole (the world's largest anole species) lying on a horizontal Ficus limb high above a busy Coral Gables (Florida) street. And that excitement was repeated only five years ago when an odd-looking baby anole collected in Lee County, Florida matured into a beautiful sail-tailed species (*Anolis ferreus*) that had not until then been recorded in the state. Today when we visit Miami, Florida, we see not only anoles of six or seven species, but brown- and yellow-banded basilisks, and other established, equally strange exotics. Virtually all of these exotics are descendants of escapees from the pet industry. Species once known only from natural history books are now common backyard and canal-edge species in southern Florida, and lizards that were once considered impossible to even keep alive in captivity are being bred with regularity by enthusiasts around the world.

Some of these lizards, the more unusual anoles, spectacular basilisks, beautiful water dragons, and the coveted sail-tailed dragons, share many husbandry needs. Today, most of us take their presence in the pet trade for granted, but they were once rarely seen and formidably expensive. As new wildlife laws are enacted, they may again become so. To assure that they do remain available, we must continue to fine-tune our herpetocultural techniques. While we do not believe the commonly offered comment that through herpetoculture uncounted species will be saved from extinction, we *do* believe that through herpetoculture one small pressure, the collecting of a species from the wild for the pet trade, can be lessened. That, in itself, makes herpetoculture more than worthwhile.

In the pages that follow we have offered comments on some of the most basic aspects, as well as on some of the more advanced procedures, pertaining to keeping anoles, basilisks, and water dragons. The comments are intended only as guidelines, as suggestions; none should be construed as the only road to success. As you become more experienced, extrapolate on our methods, devise those of your own, and share your findings.

To those of you who understand the diversity of these lizards, placing the care of anoles, basilisks, and water dragons in the same book may seem somewhat unconventional. Indeed, if looked at from a taxonomic viewpoint it *is* strange, for three separate families are represented here. The anoles are members of the family Polychrotidae, the basilisks are classified in the family Corytophanidae (both families are exclusively New World), and the water dragons are contained in the exclusively Old World family Agamidae.

But when viewed from the aspect of captive care, the approach is less incongruous. All are lizards that are found in humid, often riparian settings and some are strong swimmers. All are partially to essentially arboreal, all lay eggs that can be successfully incubated under similar conditions. In fact, except for larger cages for the bigger species and additional security for the highly nervous forms, all of these lizards thrive under similar regimens of care. Extrapolation of comments and care suggestions from one group to the next is not only possible—we encourage it.

Thus, while a discussion of these lizards in a single book may not be entirely conventional, we feel that from a herpetocultural viewpoint it does, in fact, make perfectly good sense.

We hope you will agree.

Dick & Patti Bartlett

Understanding Anoles, Basilisks, Water and Sail-tailed Dragons, and Relatives

Guidelines for All

Although the lizards in this book are now contained in three separate families they share some common characteristics. Most are at least semi-arboreal; some are persistently arboreal. Dominant males will almost invariably want a vantage perch positioned higher and in a slightly more open area than subordinate lizards. Since the body language of each family is somewhat different, representatives of all may usually be housed together, space permitting. (To stave off the possibility of cannibalism, all of the lizards should be roughly the same size.)

In many cases, you can even keep two species of the same family together with little chance of mishap; however, the keeping of two males of the same species in the same cage is usually impossible and should not be done. This statement is true even if all have been raised from hatchling size together. Sexual maturity of a male lizard basically equates to incompatibility with another sexually mature male of the same species.

How do these lizards recognize their own kind? Body language, coloration, and chemical cues (pheromones) all enter into the puzzle. We'll talk in detail in later chapters about health, breeding, and other subjects, for many species in several genera.

Stress

Many hobbyists—and not only novice hobbyists—attempt to maintain too many lizards in either too small, or incorrectly appointed, terraria. The result to the lizards is stress.

Stress does not have to be particularly overt or dramatic to prove eventually lethal to your lizards.

Some examples of stressful situations are:

- insufficient visual barriers
- too small a caging facility
- adverse extraneous stimuli
- aggression toward subordinates by dominant lizards.

The first three are easily recognizable to virtually all keepers, and they can be corrected by, respectively, the placement of additional visual barriers (such as plantings, limbs, etc.), by providing larger caging facilities or reducing the number of lizards in the present one, and by either taping an opaque shield over the glass or by moving the cage of nervous lizards into a less heavily trafficked area. On the other hand, recognizing intraspecific aggression is not always so easy, but it is every bit as critical as the more readily determined kinds of stress.

Intraspecific aggression (dominance) by these lizards can sometimes, but not always, involve actual physical conflict. The aggression can be much more subtle, yet every bit as potentially lethal. Such normal behavior by a dominant lizard as the claiming of the best basking perch, the nodding of the head, the flaring of the dewlap, or an intensification of body color, all done without actual physical contact, can and will cause a reduction in the feeding, and other responses of subordinate lizards. Males usually (but not always) interact adversely with other males, and females with other females. The larger the cage, the fewer the lizards of a single species, and the greater the number of visual barriers, the less critical these interactions may be. Be advised, however, that they can and will be used, and they can, and eventually will, take their toll.

Strange, and often not understood by the casual hobbyist, is how the presence of two males of a given species in a large cage can be debilitating when those two lizards were chosen from among a dozen, apparently non-squabbling lizards that were housed in a tiny cage at a pet dealer. The difference is that the chaos in that dealer's small tank was so great that it was impossible for *any* of the lizards to display *any* normal actions and reactions, including territoriality. It is probable that eventually the stress caused by such a situation would have been fatal to all but the strongest male and, possibly, female lizard. However, when removed from that chaos to the quasi-normalcy of an appropriate cage, the natural instincts of the lizards are again possible and are activated. Territory as well as dominance is quickly established. Lizards that appeared to have been equals in the dealer's cage become subordinates, and the stress can be channeled. A rather good rule of thumb is to house only one male and two or three

Once the shedding process begins, the skin of most lizards, like the A. carolinensis *shown, flakes off in patches.*

females of a given species in any single cage, no matter how large. In most cases, such a group will thrive.

Arm Waving

The water and the sail-tailed dragons utilize a method of arm waving (an appeasement motion) in communicating with others of their own species. Termed *circumduction* by behavioral researchers, the circular waving motion apparently appeases dominant and/or aggressive agamids toward their subordinates and is useful in establishing hierarchical positions. Circumduction is most evident in subordinate females but is not uncommonly used by hatchlings and juveniles, apparently of both sexes.

Shedding

Like snakes, as lizards grow, they periodically shed their outer skin. However, unlike snakes, which, if healthy and kept in healthy conditions, usually shed in a single, unbroken piece, the skin of most lizards (and of all of those discussed in this book) is shed in "patchwork" fashion. This is entirely normal and does not indicate an underlying problem.

Lizards shed their skin most frequently during periods of rapid growth or following injury or skin disorders. This, too, is natural, normal, and necessary.

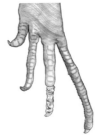

Unshed skin left on toes can lead to the loss of the toe.

The beautiful red-edged blue dewlap of the Amazonian A. nitens chrysolepis is probably as species-diagnostic to the lizards themselves as to humans.

Expect baby lizards to shed their skin more frequently than adults, and those that eat well to shed more frequently than those that don't. Lizards of all sizes shed soon after emerging from hibernation.

The Phenomenon of Natural Sunlight

Perhaps this section would be better called "the role of ultraviolet lighting," but UV is so integral to lizard behavior, and at least as important in understanding some of the mannerisms of your lizards as lighting, that the title was a toss-up.

Ultraviolet-A (UV-A) and ultraviolet-B (UV-B) are known to be important stimulants to lizards. Both are amply provided by natural, unfiltered sunlight, but only poorly so by even the best reptile sunning bulbs now available.

UV-A stimulates "natural behavior" in a lizard (or other reptile). Apparently, different strengths of UV-A stimulate differing behavior patterns, with that induced by full-strength, unfiltered sunlight being the most natural.

Is this good? Is "natural behavior" what you really want for your lizard?

Well, certainly, natural behavior is the best for a lizard. Heliothermic lizards are adapted to bask in and utilize the various rays of natural sunlight. It is under this regimen that lizards are the most alert, the most apt to breed, the best able to avoid danger, and the best able to defend themselves if caught unsuspectingly.

All of these factors seem to be impaired, at least to a small degree, when heliothermic lizards are denied access to full-strength, unfiltered, natural sunlight.

How do we know this? Well, simply approach—or try to approach—a green water dragon in the wild. First, most often, the lizard will see you long before you see it, and the only indication you'll have of its whereabouts is a thrashing in the underbrush or a splash followed by a series of ripples in a waterhole. But if you had approached and caught that lizard, you would have been bitten, scratched, and tail-whipped. This is natural behavior. For a day or two after the lizard has been taken captive, the same behavior is seen, but after a week or so, the lizard's responses dull. It no longer darts away when it is approached, and it is infinitely easier to handle when you choose to do so. "So what?" you ask. "The lizard is just getting tame. And, after all, that's exactly what we want." "Tame" lizards tend not to smash their noses up in mad dashes for freedom, nor do they rip you, the handler, to shreds.

But is your lizard truly tame?

Put that tame lizard out into the unfiltered sunlight for a day—an hour, for that matter—and watch its reversion to a truly natural behavior. It will dart away when approached, it will bite, scratch, and whip you when caught, and it will be, in every way, a wild lizard again.

If you were to leave that same lizard outside in the sunlight, but slide a pane of UV-filtering glass between it and the sun (but take care that you don't cook the lizard) within a day or two, you'd again have pretty much a tame lizard.

Similar experiments, obliterating just the UV-A, have produced similar results.

This does not mean that you can not tame a lizard. It just means that not all lizards that you think are tame, actually are, and that you should not be surprised at behavioral changes induced by natural, unfiltered sunlight.

What happens when UV-B is removed? We have now learned that when reptiles, which synthesize vitamin D_3 in their skin, are denied access to UV-B, the synthesization of this important vitamin stops. The production of D_3 is of paramount importance, for in reptiles D_3 is a calcium metabolizer. Lack of D_3 equates to an inability to metabolize calcium, even when ample calcium is present in the diet. The end result of this is the onset of metabolic bone disease. Thus, captive heliothermic (sun-basking) lizards will need both exposure to UV-A and UV-B, as well as dietary D_3 supplementation.

Although green water dragons, known scientifically as Physignathus cocincinus, *are wary and alert in the wild, in captivity most quickly lose their fear of humans.*

Hormonally Stimulated Aggression

Lizards of all species are *least* aggressive during non-breeding periods and when they are severely stressed. Conversely, they are *most* aggressive when temperatures and photoperiods dictate the advent of the breeding seasons and when they have established a territory. Males are almost invariably more territorial (at least in this grouping of lizards), hence more aggressive than females. Although in the wild, aggressive behavior is largely intraspecific (same species), in captivity aggression can occasionally be directed at very dissimilar objects. You, as your lizard's keeper, can become one of these dissimilar objects, and can become the target of aggression.

Of course, with lizards as small as most anoles, aggression would be of small concern, and even if it is a water dragon, a sudden display of aggressive behavior is more startling than dangerous. But, to have a lizard that was entirely handleable a day earlier suddenly confront a reaching hand with gaping jaws and whipping tail concerns some keepers. This behavior, too, shall pass as the breeding season ends.

Acquiring Your Lizards

Choosing a Healthy Specimen

Keeping these diverse lizards in captivity over a long period of time is a lot easier if you begin your adventure with healthy specimens. We offer you some suggestions to help you choose.

• Choose a lizard with a plump body and fleshy pelvic area. Hips or backbone protruding in bold relief are indicative of one of several underlying problems. Also ascertain that the eyes are bright and alert, have no surrounding encrustations, and are not sunken into the lizard's head. Do not mistake the cryptic behavior of arboreal lizards with lethargy; the two are entirely different.

• Ask an expert. If you are a beginning hobbyist, seek the input of a herper with more experience. Take a knowledgeable person with you when you go to pick your specimen.

Develop and keep the habit of washing your hands before and after handling your lizards.

• Select a lizard that displays an alert demeanor when disturbed but, if possible, not one that darts into the sides of its enclosure in panic.

• Choose immature specimens when possible. Better yet, choose captive-bred and -hatched specimens whenever they are available.

• Keep in mind that not all species react in the same way to the same stimulus. Learn what to expect and make your choice based on this knowledge. If you are a beginner, choose an easily kept, hardy species with which to begin your hobby.

• Ask if the lizard is handleable; some species are more readily so than others. For instance, young green water dragons are more easily handled and tamed than basilisks of similar size.

With proper care, lizards can live quite normal lifespans in captivity. For the smaller anole species, this seems to be in the four- to eight-year range, but for the larger anoles, basilisks, water dragons, and sail-tailed lizards, a lifespan can be from ten to fifteen years, or rarely, longer. Therefore, if you choose your specimen(s) carefully, and offer them the proper regimen of care, the chances are quite good that you and your chosen pet lizard will spend many years together.

Handling Do's and Don'ts

Lizards, in general, are not creatures that enjoy being restrained. Some individuals and species object to it more than others. Of the several lizard groups that we discuss in this book, it is usually only the water dragons that become tame enough to handle—and even they don't really care for it. To many lizards, being handled, being restrained, is to be subjugated—dominated. The natural instinct of any lizard is to be the *dominant*, not the dominated. So, your desire to handle and restrain your pet works against its every natural instinct. Some lizards will become quiescent and submit to handling; some won't. Those that do will often make a break for freedom at any given opportunity. We strongly suggest that you handle these lizards as little as possible, that, as we do, you enjoy them for their natural beauty and for the beauty of the terraria that you create for them.

If you *do* have to handle these lizards, be gentle but firm. When you do find it necessary to hold or restrain one of these lizards, remember that even a small specimen can and will bite, and larger types can do so painfully hard. Grip them with that in mind. With small specimens enfold neck and body in one hand. With larger specimens, enfold neck and shoulders with one hand and with the other immobilize the rear legs and give the body support.

If you are bitten, *don't rip your hand free and don't drop the lizard*. Pulling your hand sharply free can cause a more severe laceration and can tear teeth from your lizard's mouth or otherwise injure its jaws. Dropping it can result in damage to its internal organs, broken bones, or the escape of your lizard. Although arboreal species may be a little more accustomed to an occasional fall, they still should not be handled carelessly, and, should one of these tropical lizards escape in a nontropical region, the death of the lizard is a certainty with the onset of cold weather.

Claw Clipping

Large lizards with sharp claws can be uncomfortable to handle either casually as pets or just when necessary. Using fingernail clippers, the very

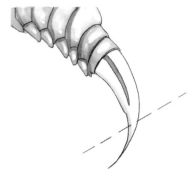

To clip the nails of your lizard, hold the foot firmly and snip off the tip with nail clippers.

tip (the tiny point that projects downward) of each claw can be removed as necessary. Do not cut into the vein that is present in each claw. Should you accidentally do so, stem the bleeding with alum or a styptic-pencil.

Sources for Obtaining Your Lizards

Pet stores. Although the more common anoles are usually readily available in pet stores across the nation and in Europe, it may be necessary to search for a specialty dealer to find the more uncommon anoles, basilisks, water and sail-tailed dragons. Such suppliers advertise in the classified sections of reptile magazines. Larger pet stores in large cities often have a more extensive reptile section than small town shops. Dealing with a local pet store has its benefits, not the least of which is being able to actually see the animal in which you are interested. Unfortunately, support information from pet store employees may not always be reliable.

Mail order. When you deal by mail order, although seeing the animal is not possible, specialty dealers are often well aware of subtle and overt needs of the species in question. Most dealers do an excellent job of portraying the animals they have on hand.

Catching a basilisk takes a steady hand and a noose or creditable running and cornering ability.

The continued existence of a mail order reptile dealer is dependent on satisfied return customers. Specialty dealers benefit from earned reputations of integrity.

Breeders. Breeders, whether specialist hobbyists or commercial breeders, are one of the best sources of parasite-free, well-acclimated specimens and accurate information. Most breeders keep records of genetics, lineage, fecundity, health, and the quirks of the specimens with which they work. These records are invariably available to their customers. Lizard breeders can be found in the classified ads of the various reptile-oriented magazines now on the market (see Useful Addresses and Information, page 92).

Shipping Information

As mentioned, there is a good chance that the specimen(s) you seek will be available only from a specialty dealer or breeder who is located some distance from you. In this case, you'll need to have the specimens you wish to purchase shipped to you by mail or air freight. For a hobbyist who has not done this before, shipping may seem intimidating, but the chances are excellent that your supplier is quite familiar with shipping and will be delighted to assist you in any way possible.

Although it is entirely legal to ship nonvenomous lizards by air mail, many dealers and breeders, because they have less control over the movement of the shipment, will not guarantee live delivery when shipping by mail. This can, and should, be an important consideration. If you elect to use air (or express) mail, do so for only the hardiest of specimens and in good weather.

Air freight is the method of transportation preferred by most dealers. It is often less convenient and more expensive than the mail service, but most dealers will guarantee live delivery (within certain parameters).

There are many things that must be considered when air transportation is involved:
1. the method of payment to be used;
2. the best time for shipment;
3. where you should have your shipment sent;
4. the best airline to use.

Let's explore some of your choices.

Payment. This should be agreed upon and fully understood at the time of ordering. You generally pay for the animal and the shipping charges in advance. It will probably be necessary to send a money order or cashier's check to the shipper, or to supply the shipper with a credit card number or wire transfer of funds to his/her account. Many shippers will accept personal checks but will not ship until the check has cleared their bank (usually within a week or so).

An alternate method of payment is COD; however, this can be expensive and inconvenient. Most airlines will accept cash only for the COD amount and there is a hefty collection fee (upwards of $15.00) in addition to all other charges.

Air shipping information. Give your supplier your full name, address, and current day and night telephone numbers where you can be reached. Inform your shipper of the airport you wish to use, or agree on a door-to-door delivery company. If your area is serviced by more than one airport (such as the Washington D.C. or San Francisco, California areas), be very specific about the airport.

Agree on a date and get the airbill number from the supplier. Avoid weekend arrivals when the cargo offices at most small airports are closed. Some shippers go to the airport on one or two specific days each week. Agree on a shipping date in advance. Allow enough time for your shipment to get to you before panicking. Most shipments take about 24 hours to get from the airport of origin to the airport of destination. It may take less time if you are lucky enough to be served by direct flights, it may take more time if you're in an area with limited flights and the shipment has to be transferred once, twice, or even more times. Keep your shipment on the same airline whenever possible; with live animals you pay for each airline involved. Ship *only* during good weather and preferably during non-peak shipping times. Your lizards may be delayed when the weather is very hot, very cold, or during the peak holiday travel/shipping/mailing times.

Level of shipping. Most airlines offer three choices: regular "space available" freight (this is the most frequently used and the suggested service level), air express (guaranteed flights), or small package (the fastest level of service). You will pay premium prices for either of the last two levels but they may be required by the airline if shipping conditions are adverse. Compare airlines; some carriers charge a lot more than others for the same level of service.

Arrival. After a reasonable time, call the airline on which your shipment is traveling and ask for the status of the shipment. The airline will need the airbill number to trace the shipment in their computer.

Pick your shipment up as quickly after its arrival as possible. This is especially important in bad weather. Find out the hours of your cargo office and whether the shipment can be picked up at the ticket counter if it arrives after the cargo office has closed.

You will have to pay for your shipment (including all COD charges and fees) before you can inspect it. Once you are given your shipment, open and inspect it *before* leaving the cargo facility.

If there's a problem. Unless otherwise specified, reliable shippers guarantee live delivery; however, to substantiate the existence of a problem, both shippers and airlines will require a "discrepancy" or "damage" report made out, *signed* and *dated* by airline personnel. In the very rare case when a problem has occurred, insist on the filling and filing of a claim form right then and contact your shipper *immediately* for instructions.

After the first time, you will no longer find shipping specimens onerous. Understanding the system will open new doors of acquisition.

Finding Your Own Lizards

Many hobbyists find seeing and catching their lizards from the wild more satisfying than purchasing them from their local pet emporiums. Some hobbyists merely pick up a pair or two of anoles while on a Florida vacation, but other hobbyists actually create their vacations around the probability of collecting anoles and other herps.

Lizards in the United States

Since it is to Florida and Latin America that many American and European vacationers travel, we have limited this chapter to the finding of lizards in these regions. Several anoles and at least one basilisk species—the northern brown—are now firmly established in Florida, but neither water dragons nor sail-trailed lizards are yet known to be found there.

"Lizard watching" tours combine observation and companionship.

Northern brown basilisks, although usually associated with quiet waters, are now common in many heavily overgrown fields and road edges in Dade County, Florida. As might be expected, the lizards are especially common along the overgrown edges of canals. Where present, these admirably camouflaged lizards may be seen at the edges of clearings, atop limestone boulders, and on low limbs in shrubby growth.

Northern brown basilisks are wary, with adult males being particularly difficult to approach. The babies are easier to approach than adults of either sex, but this is merely a comparison.

Nearly impossible to catch by hand, if approached slowly and obliquely, the diurnal, heliothermic basilisk may occasionally be caught in a long-handled field net. More often they are noosed. Gentleness and removing the lizards as quickly as possible from the noose are mandatory. Brown basilisks may occasionally be found sleeping on a limb by night. If approached stealthily, they may then be caught by hand.

Green anoles should be looked for by day as they sun on the boles of trees, telephone poles, garden fences, and similar areas. At night *A. carolinensis* may sleep on a low leaf or a blade of grass where they are easily seen by flashlight. In the warmer portions of their range (Florida and the lower Rio Grande Valley), they may be found year-round.

Brown anoles are a "low to the ground" species that can be found in shrubs, on roadside signs, fences, trash piles, fallen limbs, and tree trunks—even the walls of sheds and houses.

Other anole species can be found by heading southward to Dade and Broward Counties in Florida. To be most successful, hunt during the summer months, when even canopy species descend to lower elevations in the trees.

The little gray to pea green bark anoles, A. *distichus* ssp., are usually seen in thickets of low shrubbery. They are not uncommon near houses, but have expanded their ranges outward from urban areas along the canal systems. Tangles of bougainvillea, Surinam cherry, and crotons are favored habitats. Since these small lizards are difficult to keep in captivity, we always suggest merely looking at them. Take photographs rather than specimens.

For the knight anole, begin on a hot, humid summer morning and look for them low on the tree trunks. They hang, head down, and their yellow shoulder markings and huge pink dewlaps (both sexes have dewlaps) render them quite conspicuous. Knight anoles seem to favor broad-leafed exotic evergreen trees such as *Ficus* and *Schleffera* but may occasionally be seen in poincianas, jacarandas, and Australian pines, especially in summer when these latter trees are fully leafed.

Before you make a grab for a knight anole, remember, these lizards *bite*—and they bite *hard!* Although they will try to avoid capture, if they feel threatened and do not feel escape is possible, they will jump at your hand and bite.

Although you can now find knight anoles all over Miami and surrounding towns, they seem particularly common in Coral Gables where they may be seen on Ficus trees used in median plantings.

The Jamaican giant anole, A. garmani, is a big anole that looks superficially like a gigantic green anole. It can be found in some of the larger trees in Dade and Lee counties. The males can exceed a foot in length and because of their newness in the wilds of urban Florida, these pretty anoles are currently more coveted than the larger knight anoles. Many homeowners take a protective attitude toward these bright green, nonagressive lizards.

Jamaican giants seem to descend lower in the trees during the hot, humid days of summer. They are often seen in large jacaranda and poinciana trees when the trees are sparsely leafed in winter. Spotting them when the trees have full foliage is just about impossible. Where they are persecuted by collectors for the pet trade, the lizards become very wary.

The Puerto Rican crested anole, A. c. cristatellus, was found several years ago in Dade County, Florida. Like the brown anole, with which it might be confused, the crested anole usually positions itself low on tree trunks, fences, trash piles, etc. Crested anoles are now widespread and common in southern Dade County.

Lizards in Other Countries

There are times when your vacation may take you out of the United States, or, if you are an avid and advanced herper, you may actually plan a vacation that allows you to see certain species of reptiles and amphibians in the field. Remember that your visit must legally be restricted to only seeing and perhaps photographing the animals in the wild. Permits are needed if you plan to collect them, export them from the country of origin, or import them to the United States.

Many anoles and basilisks of three kinds may be found in Costa Rica, a popular vacation destination.

A. nitens chrysolepis *is another of many species of cryptically colored anoles. When not moving, the lizards are very difficult to see amid the litter on the forest floor.*

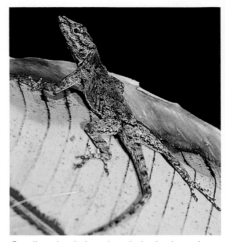

Small and quietly colored, the bark anole, A. distichus *ssp. is more difficult to keep successfully than other anole species.*

On a recent trip to the Peruvian Amazon, among the 90 some species of reptiles and amphibians found, we were fortunate enough to see six species of anoles. Unlike the anoles in the United States, which are often numerous, we searched long and hard for the few specimens we did find. While some were seen during the daylight hours, the sightings occurred only after extended hikes, often in driving rains. Others, among these the beauti-

ful *A. transversalis*, were found by flashlight at night, again usually after long, muddy hikes that took us deep into the rainforests.

A. transversalis is a large, beautiful, and sexually dimorphic species. No matter what their ground color, the females we saw were prominently marked with the broad transverse bands from which their specific name is derived. Even their rather small, off-white or light yellow dewlap was trans-

The adult male (left) of the yellow-dewlapped A. transversalis *is less prominently barred than the female (right).*

A. biporcatus *is one of the more common arboreal anoles of Central America. It can change its color from green to brown.*

A. extremus, *a species of moderate size and complex coloration, is occasionally imported from Barbados for the American pet trade.*

versely banded with dark spots. While the body bands of the males were discernible, they had been infiltrated with dark specks and flecks and were poorly defined. The variably colored but often yellow dewlap of adult males is immense. It extends rearward to mid venter. Like most other anoles that assume a green coloration, *A. transversalis* is highly arboreal. The several specimens of the 10-inch-long (25 cm) anole that we saw were all found at varying heights in rainforest trees.

We found two other anole species on or near the forest floor, among the fallen leaves that camouflaged them admirably. Both were shade-dwelling brown species that attain about 7 inches (17.8 cm) in total length. These were the robust and angular *A. bombiceps* and the very similar and sympatic *A. nitens chrysolepis*. The two differ in very minimal ways, but the dewlaps of the *A. bombiceps* we found were predominantly blue, while those of the *A. n. chrysolepis* were blue-centered,

The Amazonian A. bombiceps *is another species that blends remarkably with the fallen leaves on the forest floor.*

Rather than an intense green, captive knight anoles are often of a pretty bluish-green coloration. This may be due to the lack of trace elements in their diet.

red-edged, and bore numerous white(ish) scales in the blue field when distended.

Three smaller, brownish species were also found. Although the first of these, the pale brown *A. aurofuscata* was not uncommon on the isolated clearing trees along the various river banks, the other two seemed of more terrestrial habits. Even the dewlap of *A. aurofuscatus* was pale and varied from reddish to almost yellow. Those we observed were alert and difficult to approach, darting upward from the trunk to the foliage as we neared. This is a small anole species, averaging about 5 inches (12.7 cm) in length.

The single *A. ortonii* that we found was an adult female. She was clad in a pale tannish gray and bore a vague, irregular, lineate pattern on her sides and back. The average-sized dewlap of the male can vary from yellow-orange to a rather bright red, or can even be bicolored.

The final species we saw was the rather inconspicuous *A. trachyderma*. It has a variable brown dorsum and a variable (orange-yellow to orange-red) dewlap and was found low on clearing trees and fallen, forest-edge leaf litter.

The difficulty we experienced in finding these six South American species, as well as the similarities in the appearance of many of them and the remarkable camouflage provided by their cryptic coloration, explains why additional species of anole continue to be found by researchers. All of these occur from ground level to rather low in the trees where they are more or less easily seen. It would be much more difficult to find the various canopy species.

Caging

Determining the most satisfactory caging for a lizard may take some thought. The kind of cage used will vary according to the amount and type of space you have available. Where will you be keeping your lizards? Will you keep them indoors in a limited space, indoors in a more spacious area, on your outdoor patio, or elsewhere?

Outdoor Caging Suggestions

We find keeping lizards outdoors infinitely more satisfying than keeping them in small indoor terraria. Although at some latitudes keeping them outside would be only a summer option (and then only with nighttime heat from above-cage heat bulbs), when and where possible we strongly suggest outdoors maintenance. We try always to provide a cage large enough for a breeding colony. To provide us opportunity to interact with the lizards, we construct the cages in a way that allows us easy entry. We call them "step-in" or "walk-in" cages.

Caging Basics

The smallest of our outside cages measures 48 inches long × 30 inches wide × 72 inches high (122 cm × 76 cm × 183 cm). The larger cages are of similar width and height but are 96 inches (244 cm) long. All are on large casters (wheels) to facilitate easy moving. The uprights of the frames and the door assembly (which measures 2 feet × 4 feet [5.1 cm × 10.2 cm]) are made from 2 × 2 lumber. The top and bottom are solid pieces of marine plywood. The top has had the center removed, leaving a rim about 6 inches (15 cm) wide all the way around. The sides, front, back, door, and top are covered with ⅛-inch (3.18 mm) mesh welded hardware cloth that is stapled tightly in place. The 30-inch (76 cm) width and the 72-inch (183 cm) height (which includes the casters) allow these cages to be easily wheeled through average interior and exterior doorways. Although it may take some effort, the cages can therefore be wheeled inside during inclement weather, or outside on pleasant days to allow the lizards natural sunlight and rain. The cage furniture consists of a full-cage-height Ficus tree (usually *F. benjamina*) and a number of dead limb perches of suitable diameter.

Cage Sizes

While the large (step-in) cages described above are our preference, especially for the water dragons, basilisks, and larger anoles, we have used smaller cages equally well for both large and small species. We have successfully kept small anoles and babies of the larger lizard species in caging as small as a 10-gallon (37.8 L) terraria. Adults of the various basilisks and water dragons should be in 55-gallon (208 L) show tanks. We always incorporate some type of potted plant as well as horizontal perching limbs into the decor. Smaller wood and wire cages that offer greater ventilation than converted aquaria can also be constructed. In the high humidity of Florida, we actually prefer the former.

Vertical Caging

A cage containing a pair or trio of Jamaican giant or knight anoles

Where and when climatic conditions allow, outside cages of wood and wire construction are ideal for most lizards.

should measure about 4 feet long × 2.5 feet wide × 6 feet high (1.22 m × 0.76 m × 1.83 m). A cage containing more than that number should be about 6 feet × 2.5 feet × 6 feet (1.83 m × 0.76 m × 1.83 m).

Horizontal Caging

We provide vertically oriented terraria/cages for arboreal species, but for lizards that are more terrestrial we strive to offer a proportionately greater amount of horizontal space. By using ⅛-inch (3.18 m) mesh in the cage construction, we prevent the escape of all but the smallest food insects.

Indoor Caging Suggestions

Many enthusiasts actually begin keeping reptiles because they have neither time, space, nor ability to keep a dog, cat, or bird. This is especially true of apartment and condo dwellers, many of whom are faced with regulations prohibiting so-called "normal"

pets. Reptiles of many kinds can, on the other hand, be kept in enclosed indoor quarters. If certain conditions are met by their keepers, lizards, too, can be satisfying, long-lived, indoor pets, but be advised that the vivaria for most lizards will need more thought and somewhat more sophisticated equipment than would the terrarium for a snake.

Anoles, basilisks, and water dragons are among the types of lizards that are often first chosen by hobbyists. All can and will thrive indoors. Since most anoles are small and highly arboreal, they can be kept in proportionately tall terraria of rather small lateral dimensions. The larger size and more active horizontal lifestyle of basilisks and water dragons dictate that these creatures be provided with proportionately more terrarium floor space. Adequate height is also important.

In the wild, the arboreal anole species currently available in the American pet trade may alter their preferred microhabitats by season (and/or ambient temperature). For example, the impressive knight anole, *A. equestris*, may remain high in the canopy where thermoregulation is relatively easy during the cooler months of the year. When ambient temperatures warm to or above its preferred minimum (thus making thermoregulation largely unnecessary), the big lizard descends the trunks to just a few feet above the ground. We have noticed the same tendency with the Jamaican giant anole, *A. garmani*, but rather than remaining in the dense canopy, during the winter this species tends to bask high on the trunks and upper branches of seasonally sparsely leaved trees (such as poinciana and jacaranda). Jamaican giant anoles also descend to about head level on tree trunks during the warmer months. When captive, anoles seem to fare better in vertically oriented cages.

Stacked Cages

To dwell contentedly indoors, we believe that anoles require vertically oriented cages. These can be either custom-made (an expensive way to go) or constructed by stacking two, three, or even four aquaria of identical size into a tower. This method is usually considerably less expensive than a custom-built terrarium, but cost varies dramatically according to the gallonage/size of the tanks used.

Exactly what do we mean by a "stacked terrarium," how do we go about making it, and of what benefit would this be? Well, let's explore the combinations possible with standard 20-gallon (75.7 L) "long" tanks. Let's say you've found just enough space for a 20-gallon (75.7 L) aquarium stand in your living room (the dimensions of a single tank are 30 inches long × 12 inches wide × 12 inches high [76 cm × 30.5 cm × 30.5 cm]—the stand is slightly larger). The length and width are adequate for a pair of green, or other small, anole species. The height would also probably suffice, but the anoles would be happier with additional climbing room. So, you purchase a second 20-gallon (75.7 L) long tank and invert it on top of the first one. Although taking up no more of your valuable floor area, this addition has given your anoles exactly twice the volume of usable space. This is economy that is hard to beat. Three or even four times the original volume can be provided by stacking a third, or a third and a fourth, tank between the bottom and the top one.

Removing the bottom. Of course, each tank comes with a bottom, the removal of which becomes mandatory when the stacking system is used. To do this, take the tank(s) to a quiet area, and set them, bottomside down, on a flat surface that is covered with newspaper. Cover the inside surface of the bottom thickly with newspaper, then tap the bottom soundly with a hammer. Using extreme care, remove all pieces of loose and broken glass. Dispose of this properly, and be very careful of stray shards when you are working and removing the broken glass. Remember also, when you again handle the tank, that once the bottom is removed from a tank, the tank loses much of its structural integrity. Handle such tanks *very* gently and *very* cautiously!

Stacking. Once in place, the tanks in the stack can be held in place in one or two ways. The more temporary of the two is by wrapping two frames together with a high-quality, wide, transparent plastic tape. Running a bead of latex aquarium sealant along the top of one frame before setting the next tank up top of it is somewhat more permanent.

Maintenance. Keep in mind that servicing a tall tank is more difficult than servicing a low one. It may be necessary to use a stepstool or other such item to reach a height where servicing the tank is possible.

The servicing of stacked terraria can be made easier by affixing the tape to only the rear of the mid-level terrarium and tilting the top section backwards when you need access. We do this by keeping the stack out a foot or so from the wall and tilting the top section back until the stack rests securely against the wall. You can then easily clean the tank or feed or water the lizards through the V-shaped opening created by the tilted top.

Humidity. Excessive humidity may be a concern in some regions or during some seasons and may become a paramount concern when living plants are used in terraria. Using a commercial screen top will help. If the tank becomes too dry, adding a piece of plexiglass to the screen top will help hold moisture inside the tanks.

HOW-TO:
Building an Outdoor Cage

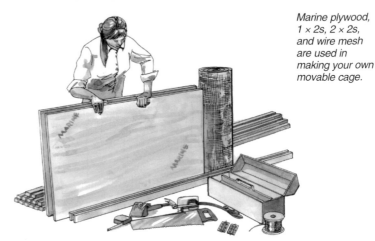

Marine plywood, 1 × 2s, 2 × 2s, and wire mesh are used in making your own movable cage.

Although neither of us is a gifted carpenter, we do enjoy building our own cages.

Our outside cages reside in sunlit splendor on a wooden deck. We build all of our cages as large as feasibly possible, since we intend them to be used year-round. We also proportion them so that they can be rolled inside. If the cage you are intending to build will be used only during the warmth of summer (taking the lizards indoors during cool/cold weather), movability and dimensions will be less critical.

With that in mind, we suggest that you first determine how much space you have. Besides determining how big the finished cage will be, the available space should help you decide what kind (or at least what size range) of lizards you'll be keeping. The following instructions and material list enable you to build a cage (with rounded corners) approximately 32 inches wide, 48 inches long, and 72 inches high (81.3 cm × 122 cm × 183 cm) (plus caster height). By not rounding the corners of the bottom and top, you can cut down considerably on your work as well as reduce by four the number of 2 × 2s needed.

Materials

The materials you will need are as follows:
• Two pieces of ¾-inch (19.1 mm) thick marine plywood, 32 inches × 48 inches (81 cm × 122 cm)

• Straight 2 × 2s (we use treated lumber and have never had any problems). You'll need at least 13 eight-footers (2.4 m)
• Thin wooden or galvanized facing strips to face the inside of the door opening
• ⅛-inch (3.18 mm) mesh welded wire hardware cloth. We buy ours by the roll in 36-inch (91 cm) heights. You will need about 30 feet (9.1 m) per cage.
• Galvanized nails
• A few feet of thin, pliable, single-strand wire
• Staples
• Two sturdy hinges and two hooks and eyes
• Saw, hammer, staple gun, tape measure or yardstick, and screwdriver

Since our building methods are not precise, we precut only the 10 upright braces to 5 feet 10 inches (177.8 cm) in length and the plywood top and bottom. Horizontal braces and door are measured and cut to exact length or size as we build.

Top and Bottom of the Cage

We first tackle the top and the bottom of the cage. Because of the constant high humidity and frequent rains in Florida, we use marine plywood of ¾-inch (19.1 mm) thickness for both top and bottom. The dimensions we have settled on for most cages are 32 inches × 48 inches (81.3 cm × 122 cm). We round the corners (this is optional), using an arc on an 8-inch (20 cm) diameter. Exactly the same arc must be used to round the corners of both bottom and top (we use a salad plate). Once the corners are rounded (optional), the bottom is done; however, we cut a sizable panel out of the center of the top (we usually leave a 6-inch [15.2 cm] rim on all sides and remove the rest). The hole left by the removed panel is, of course, screened.

We build the cage while it is lying on its back, first nailing the inner two uprights in place. Once those are secure, we roll the cage onto a side and nail the next two, and so on. Note that the front door has four uprights, the door hanging between the innermost two.

We build and screen the door before hanging it. We have found that a width of 2 feet (0.6) and a height of 4 feet (1.2 m) is adequate for the door. The frame is made from 2 × 2s.

Finishing the Cage

Because the ⅛-inch (3.18 m) hardware cloth we use is in 3-foot (0.9 m) heights, and we run it horizontally, horizontal cross braces are necessary between the main uprights. These are positioned about 2 feet 11 inches (88.9 cm) below the top (or above the bottom) of the cage.

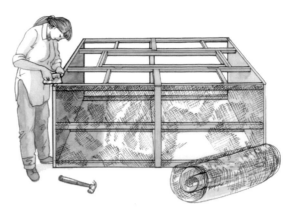

Place the cage on its back to staple the wire mesh in place.

The wire is overlapped slightly and stapled along both its top and bottom edges. The overlapping wire is then laced together with pliable single-strand wire along all of the corner arcs. Be sure the hardware cloth is pulled tightly when it is applied and that "puckers," if any, are folded tightly and secured.

Stacked aquariums, taped at the junctures, make an accessible and inexpensive type of vertical housing.

Stabilizing the tanks. Placing a horizontal brace that doubles as a planter in each tank from which the bottom has been removed will help to stabilize the tank. The brace, a simple cross piece of glass of the desired size, can be securely held in place by aquarium sealant. Each of these braces can be fronted with a low piece of glass, also held in place by sealant. Atop these fronted braces, you can plant some humidity-tolerant vining plants such as philodendron or Epipremnum (=pothos). The presence of the vines will beautify your terrarium and serve as areas of security for the lizards.

Stacked tank cage furniture. Whether it consists of only two, or four, or more tanks, at some point you may wish to dismantle the stacked tanks, even if only temporarily for a thorough cleaning.

If the cage furniture used in each tank of the stacked arrangement is kept separate, the dismantling will be considerably easier.

Rather than running branches vertically from bottom to top of the arrangement, zigzag them diagonally upwards from corner to corner within the same tank. Have the top of one branch meet the bottom of another in the tank below or above. This will provide easy climbing and a multitude of basking areas for your anoles, but allow each tank to be lifted free of the one below without undue disturbance.

Adding plants. Vining plants are recommended, and we strongly suggest that you have these in the corner of each tank. If the plants are affixed near the top of the terrarium, trim the vining stems back when they get too long (or at least be prepared to do so if necessary). Although you don't want the individual tanks to look like separate entities, the more discrete (self-contained) each tank in the stack is, the easier the dismantling and cleaning will be when it becomes necessary.

Vertically Oriented Tanks

Using one tank. Easier, perhaps, than the stacking of tanks, is the purchasing of one large one (55- to 100-gallon [189–378.5 L] sizes are perfect), orienting it vertically and glassing (or otherwise closing) in the top, which has now become a side. To facilitate the usage of a commercial top, it will be necessary to keep the frame of the tank at least one-half inch (12.7 mm) above the surface on which it sits. This can be accomplished by placing a number of rubber stoppers, which can be purchased in hardware stores, between the stand and the tank.

Closing the open side. It can actually be closed in any one of several ways. Commercial tops are available for most aquarium sizes. These can be clipped into place but when they are used, the whole side opens at once for access. While such a large opening certainly provides easy access for cleaning, it also assures nervous lizards an easy avenue of escape. It is much safer to have the access to the open side divided into two, or even three, separate entry panels with at least one—the bottom—being glass. The glass panel can be held firmly and tightly in place by a continuous bead of aquarium sealant on the two sides and the bottom. A screen top can be clipped into place on top of the glass panel; just make sure that you've taped the open edge of the glass so you don't cut yourself when you reach into the tank.

Horizontally Oriented Tanks for Basilisks and Water Dragons

Tanks for runners. Some of these lizards will do well in terraria oriented in precisely the way they were designed to be oriented—horizontally. Those lizards are the four species of basilisks and two species of water dragons.

Because of their active lifestyles, basilisks and water dragons should be given the largest possible cages. We suggest a minimum size of 100 gallons (378.5 L)—and preferably twice that—for a pair of adult specimens.

Visual barriers. Many basilisks, and to a somewhat lesser degree, water dragons, are nervous and quick to take fright. This is especially true of wild-collected specimens. These lizards, unused to transparent restraints (such as glass) in the wild, may continually batter their noses in their efforts to escape. A profusion of visual barriers in their cages, such as horizontal and diagonal limbs and vining vegetation (either real or artificial), may help these lizards feel more secure. You should always move slowly when you are near the vivarium.

Even with visual barriers and slow movement, we have, in many cases, found it necessary to tape sheets of paper or plasticized backings over most of the glass surfaces of the cage. These opaque barriers not only provide the lizards with additional security,

To open a stacked aquarium system, remove the tape and tilt the top tank back to rest against the wall.

but enable them to know when they are near the edges of their vivarium, resulting in less nose battering. As the lizards have become used to our presence, we have, over time, been able to remove most, or all, of the paper shields. The red-headed basilisk, *Basiliscus galeritus*, has proven the most consistently nervous of all six species. The constant nervous

Use aquarium sealant to attach a brace which also serves as a plant shelf.

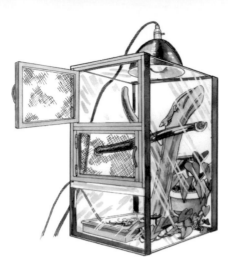

An aquarium can be turned on its side to provide a vertical format cage for a smaller lizard such as an anole.

vigilance and immediate flight response of this lizard species has caused us to maintain them in nearly complete visual seclusion while captive.

Basking. Basilisks and water dragons enjoy basking well above ground level

The horizontal format wood and wire cage provides an active lizard such as a basilisk room to roam, but make sure there are enough visual barriers to make the lizard feel secure.

on thick, sun- (or lamp-) warmed, horizontal limbs. Sufficient perches should be provided for *all* specimens, or only the dominant lizard will use a perch.

Cage Furniture and Accessories for Horizontally Oriented Tanks

"Naturalistic" caging. One of the things we like best about keeping these interesting lizards is that they do better in brightly lit, beautifully planted, botanically interesting facilities than in the starkness so often associated with the cages used by American herpetoculturists. Vining plants, bromeliads, small orchids, or other plant species that thrive in high humidity situations can be used singly or in combination, and lichened limbs, mosses, and attractively shaped colored and arranged rocks are all sought by vivarists.

Plants. Among the vining plants, several of the philodendrons and pothos are excellent choices. All thrive under reduced light and in high humidity situations. Non-vining (also called "self-heading") forms of philodendrons and anthuriums also do well. Small species of bromeliads (air plants) can be positioned either in the soil or wired onto limbs, where, if misted occasionally and given sufficient light, they will thrive and vegetatively multiply. Small epiphytic orchids can accompany the bromeliads on elevated boughs and if conditions are suitable, some of the hardiest forms will multiply and bloom. Old limbs, most festooned with arboreal ferns and/or lichens, are strewn on our woodland floor. We utilize some of the prettier ones in our terraria.

Rocks and perches. Pitted (oolitic) limestone rocks and boulders are found all over Florida, and other kinds of rock formations, some mossy, some lichenate, some simply pretty in their stratifications, can be gathered in other parts of the world. Hobbyists can find rocks, manzanita, cholla (cactus) skeletons, and other decorations in pet stores. Rocky formations seem less desirable for these lizards than limbs, but may certainly be incorporated into the overall vivarium setups. We caution you to be sure that, when rocks are used, they are placed firmly and cannot shift position—even if your lizards should try to burrow beneath them.

Positioning perches. Anoles like their perches high up in their terraria and most will preferentially choose to bask on a horizontal or diagonal perch rather than a vertical (or nearly vertical) one. Smaller species also readily use leaves and grasses as perching and sleeping stations. Horizontal or diagonal perches can be held in place wherever you want them in the terrarium by simply placing a suitably wide and deep U-shaped bead of aquarium sealant (open side up) on the glass ends of the tank and, once the sealant has dried, dropping the limb into place.

Although adept climbers, basilisks and water dragons preferentially bask at levels lower than those chosen by most anoles.

Although even large anole species will occasionally climb on yielding twig tips, they, and the basilisks and water dragons, prefer perches of at least the diameter of their bodies. In community (multi-lizard) setups, several equally prominent perches are better than a single one. This is especially true when the community setups involve more than a single species, each with its single dominant male.

Substrate. The substrate of your terrarium may be as varied as the furniture. Although it is not particularly aesthetic (especially in an otherwise "naturalistic" setup), layers of newspaper or paper towelling can be used on the bottom. These have the advantage of being absorbent, inexpensive, readily available, and easily changed. Should you choose, a layer of fallen leaves can be gathered up and spread over the paper. We usually use only a thick layer

Brace your wooden climbing logs by anchoring them to a wide base.

of fallen leaves. Because they are durable and easy to work with, we use the leaves of live oaks, *Quercus virginiana* in our terraria, replacing them with new when necessary.

Hide boxes. Basilisks (occasionally) and water dragons (frequently) will use hiding areas if they are provided. Easily cleaned and sterilized plastic

Use a variety of plants and wood pieces to add visual barriers to your cage.

Accomplished aerialists, young green basilisks clamber animatedly through the plants in their cages. Larger basilisks would choose elevated limbs.

Tape paper over the end of the cage, halfway up or cover the entire side. Use a drape over the front to accustom a flighty lizard to the clear glass.

caves—some incorporating water dishes in their designs—are stocked by many pet shops.

Anoles prefer elevated hiding areas. A hollowed or slotted limb or a piece of hollowed cholla cactus skeleton sus-

Anoles are ideal lizards for "naturalistic" indoor terraria.

pended near the top of the terrarium will usually be used extensively by these treetop sprites.

Such items as "hot rocks" and "heat limbs" are available, but we do not encourage their use (see comments in heating and lighting sections, pages 30–32).

Cagemates

Although the anoles, basilisks and water dragons are not as solitary as some lizards, the males are still highly territorial. It is usually impossible—and never particularly desirable—to keep more than a single sexually mature male of a given species, or of a closely allied species, in each cage. Intraspecific aggression among males can be persistent and fatal. If not crowded, you may usually keep from one to several adult females with each male. Although the females are usually somewhat less aggressive toward each other, hierarchies may be formed. You must ascertain that all subordinate specimens continue to feed and drink adequately, be allowed to bask, and are

28

not unduly stressed by the dominant female. Juveniles of both sexes can be housed together, although growth may be more rapid if only a single specimen is kept per container.

Given a large enough cage, it may be possible to keep two diverse species of anoles, such as a green and a brown, or another combination of these lizards, together. For instance, we have successfully kept knight anoles and green basilisks together, and have seen brown basilisks kept with green water dragons. In neither combination did the two species show the slightest interest in each other. Other combinations are equally possible. Experiment, but watch closely for adverse reactions. We have successfully kept compatibly-sized day geckos, White's and other large treefrogs, and a fair number of other nonaggressive lizard species caged with anoles, basilisks, and water dragons.

Thermoregulation

Every reptile has a body temperature at which all daily functions are optimized; lizards are no exception to this rule. Like other reptiles, lizards attain this preferred temperature by thermoregulation. Thermoregulation—the altering of body temperature by external means—can mean either warming or cooling, as necessary, and can be accomplished in various ways. Certain lizards, especially nocturnal and/or high-altitude forms, may lay on top of or beneath sun-warmed rocks or logs. To cool themselves, they merely move away from the warmed object against which they have been lying. Lizards that thermoregulate in this manner are termed *thigmothermic*. However, most lizards, at least most with which hobbyists are familiar, are *heliothermic*. That means, to warm themselves, these lizards seek sun-warmed/sunlit areas in which to bask. They are physiologically adapted to

Water dragons like to bask on sturdy limbs above water.

being warmed primarily from above. Although the little casque-headed lizards of the genus *Corytophanes* seem to indulge in heliothermic behavior less than most others, most anoles and relatives, basilisks and relatives, and water dragons are heliotherms.

Warm from Above

Because they *are* heliotherms, we recommend that the anoles, basilisks,

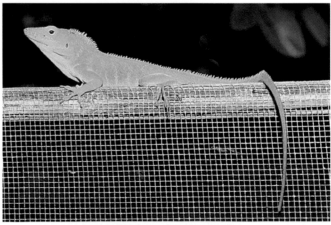

Wild Jamaican giant anoles in our yard would often bask atop the cages in which other anole species were housed.

A variety of methods can be used to heat and light your cages.

and water dragons be warmed, as well as illuminated naturally, from above. We strongly feel that warmth-producing flood- and spotlights directed onto/into basking areas (either preferred areas of the terrarium floor or a limb near the cage top) are much more satisfactory for thermoregulation than are the electrified artificial limbs and rocks now available.

Bulb Wattage

Vary the bulb wattage of the bulb(s) according to terrarium size. Basking temperatures for most of these lizards can be maintained in a 10-gallon (37.85 L) terrarium by a 50-watt plant floodlight, especially if it is directed toward a tank-top limb. Heating an area on the terrarium floor might require the more directed rays of a spotlight bulb. Attaining the same suitable temperatures in a stacked 100-gallon (378.5 L) terrarium may require a 150- or 200-watt bulb. Suitably heating the terrarium will require smaller bulbs in warm conditions than in cooler ones.

Caution: The directed rays of even a rather small bulb can easily melt the plastic now used on aquarium frames. The heat from large bulbs can even break aquarium glass. Too large a bulb

can overheat your terrarium and the high temperatures can be lethal to your lizards. Also, rays from misdirected or oversized bulbs can burn and kill plant leaves. When using lights or heaters of any kind, *always use extreme care!*

Temperatures

Anoles, basilisks, and water dragons like warm temperatures and high relative humidity. Although species from the forest floor may be adapted to cooler temperatures (but higher humidity) than the forest-edge and savanna species, the variance is by only a very few degrees. Species from high altitudes (of which there are currently few in the pet trade) may be adapted to colder nighttime lows than lowland species, but would still thermoregulate extensively during their daytime hours of activity.

Suggestions for preferred habitat and temperature range are provided in the species account section of this book (see pages 60–88). If you are not sure what temperature your species prefers, we suggest erring slightly on the side of warmth.

Day Versus Night

A cage that is maintained in the high 80s°F (27–32°C) by day and in the low 70s°F (31–23°C) or high 60s°F (19–31°C) by night will prove ideal for most anoles and for all basilisks and water dragons. Except for forest floor species, a high level of full-spectrum illumination is desirable. Provide a warmed basking area (surface temperature of about 95°F [38.8°C]) during the hours of daylight by prudent use of a floodlight. Many anoles preferentially bask while positioned head downward on a tree trunk. Other anoles and the basilisks and water dragons may bask on a horizontal limb, on top of thick vegetation, or on the ground. Accommodate all possibilities by providing suitably sized limbs positioned both vertically and horizontally.

The actual heating may be accomplished in several ways.

Area warming. The method that we most favor for area warming is by the prudent use of directed bulbs (flood or spot). Undertank heaters, used in conjunction with directed overhead lighting, may also be useful. Such heaters, made specifically for this purpose, are available in most pet shops. Human heating pads may also be adapted as undertank heaters. Be advised that the use of an undertank heater beneath the water receptacle may lethally overheat the water and will assuredly increase cage humidity. A few degrees of warmth and additional humidity can be gained by placing an aquarium heater in a tall, slim jar of water and taping the jar in place in a not easily seen corner of the tank. If you do use this method, be sure that your lizards cannot purposely or accidentally enter the jar and drown or jostle and break the heater. Add only warm-to-hot water to replace the evaporated water, or the temperature change will break the heater sheath.

The wood and wire cage on casters is easy to move.

Hibernation

Of all of the species mentioned in these pages, hibernation (also called brumation), a period of winter dormancy, could be considered for only two: North American green anoles, *Anolis carolinensis*, from the northernmost populations, and the southern-temperate Australian (or brown) water dragon, *Physignathus lesueurii*, from the southernmost populations. Since it is difficult, or impossible, to ascertain the origin of any given specimen once it has entered the pet trade, it is probably best to not consider hibernation for pet specimens of either. If you wish to *breed* your water dragons, use extreme caution (see HOW-TO: Hibernating the Brown Water Dragon, pages 54–55).

Lighting

Outside Caging

If you are using outside cages of wood and wire construction, properly lighting and heating them will be a simple matter during the late spring, summer, and early fall months in most temperate climes. For those of us in southern Florida or the lower Rio Grande Valley in Texas, it should be relatively easy year round. Simply wheel or carry your cages to a sunny spot outdoors and let nature take its course. Natural, unfiltered sunlight is the best of all possible lighting, providing the normal, beneficial amounts of UV-A and UV-B, and warmth for the animal.

On the other hand, glass terraria will not only filter out most of the beneficial UV-A and UV-B rays, but even on a cool day glass will concentrate the rays of the sun, causing your terrarium to quickly, and lethally, overheat.

Even small anoles, such as this hatchling large-headed anole, may bite if they feel threatened.

flood lamp (we use plant-grow bulbs for this function, but full-spectrum (actually color-corrected) incandescents are now available) as well as full-spectrum fluorescent lighting. The latter provides your specimens with at least some UV-A and UV-B. Although the necessity of ultraviolet rays in reptile husbandry still needs additional research, the full-spectrum fluorescent bulbs do seem to induce a rather normal activity pattern, and just may assist reptiles in synthesizing vitamin D_3, or at least in metabolizing calcium. Certainly, you should do everything possible to provide your captive lizards with the conditions that best promote the most normal life and lifestyle.

Inside Caging

Proper lighting is very important to the well-being of your lizards. Heliothermic (sun-basking) lizards require proper illumination to induce activity. This is true even when conditions are otherwise optimum. Forest species may require slightly less light than those from more open settings.

Indoor caging facilities should be provided with both a heat-producing

Greenhouses

Bigger Is Better

As hobbyists progress from novice to advanced status, many decide that they truly enjoy the hobby of reptile keeping and expand the scope of their hobbies in many ways. Some expand collections and some may specialize but delve more deeply into the natural history or the reproductive biology of the species in which they have developed the most interest. Often, both schools decide that they would like bigger and better facilities.

What could be bigger and better than a reptile-dedicated greenhouse? While it is certainly true that greenhouses are a luxury item, they are more in vogue today than ever before. And, like other caging facilities, they can be purchased in either a kit or pre-built product, or they can be homemade. They can be simply elaborate, or elaborately simple. In many areas, greenhouses are considered permanent structures and a building permit is required to legally install one.

Anoles, basilisks, water and sail-tailed dragons, and their allies, are ideal greenhouse lizards. They all

An add-on greenhouse is a functional and attractive home for your lizards.

thrive in highly humid, lushly planted situations. They may be either kept caged inside the greenhouse, or let loose to roam the entire structure. We favor the latter concept. However, all lizards are far more adept at escaping their caging facilities than even the most agile of plants, and the glass-climbing anoles are especially so. The lizard greenhouse must be secure in every aspect, and should have double-entry doors as an enhanced containment system. Windows and ventilators, either low or along the ridgepole, must be tightly screened from the inside. Heating and cooling units must be entirely screened to prevent injury to the lizards.

The dark brown post-orbital stripe so apparent on all but the very youngest brown water dragons, is particularly well defined on the adult male.

Building a Greenhouse

Building a greenhouse is fun. While securing it as a lizard house can be tedious, the end result will provide you with years of satisfaction.

When landscaped with imagination, the interior of even a small greenhouse can be your own bit of rainforest habitat and, as such, can provide a healthy and secure habitat for your lizards that could not be otherwise attained.

Landscaping

Rock formations and waterfalls may be bedecked with mosses, ferns, selaginellas, and episcias, small sunken ponds be replete with blooming tropical water lilies, while lush growths of philodendrons, epipremnums, and syngoniums create secure tangles. Weathered tree skeletons may be used for perches—only your imagination and your pocketbook will limit the possibilities.

Construction tips. We suggest that the base be sunk a foot (0.3 m) or more below the surface of the ground and that whenever possible, insulating, double glazing be used. We learned that the higher cost of the latter is quickly offset by the ease (and savings) with which the finished structure may be heated or cooled.

Feeding and Watering Your Lizards

Getting Started

Anoles, basilisks, water dragons, and their relatives are primarily insectivores, but larger specimens of some larger species will also eat small mice, fruit/honey mixtures, blossoms, and some other plant materials. Captives can be acclimated to feed on insects or rodents that are easily available to us.

Getting the lizard to feed for the first time may not be easy. A lizard deprived of food for a lengthy period by collector or wholesaler may need considerable prodding to begin feeding again. This is especially true of cone-headed and casque-headed lizards that dehydrate and stress easily and quickly. Offering a variety of foods in secure and calming surroundings will,

Anoles, basilisks, and water and sail-tailed dragons in captivity feed upon crickets, meal worms (both types), house flies and wax worms.

with luck, tempt your lizard into feeding. Once it has begun feeding again, it is likely that it will continue to do so, and it may even expand its horizons to a food type quite different from the one that is natural to it.

Insects

Nothing is ever quite so easy as it initially seems! So your lizards eat insects—what could be easier to provide? But, you will quickly learn that there's more to feeding insects to your lizards than just tossing a few odd crickets into the cage. You have to feed your insects well before you offer them to your amphibians. Caring properly for your feed insects is an important aspect of successful herpetological husbandry. A poorly fed or otherwise unhealthy insect offers little but bulk when fed to a reptile; therefore, offering food insects in top-notch health should be a main concern of any herpetoculturist.

Feeding Insects

The term "gut-loading" as in "G-L crickets" is used to indicate insects that are fed highly nutritious foods immediately before being offered as food. Calcium, vitamin D_3, fresh fruit and vegetables, fresh alfalfa and/or bean sprouts, honey and vitamin/mineral-enhanced (chick) laying mash are only a few of the foods that may be considered for gut-loading insects. A commercially prepared gut-loading diet has only recently reached the pet marketplace. Insects quickly lose much of their food value if not continually fed an abundance of highly nourishing food. Most insects eat continually, so it is much to the benefit of your lizards if you supply the insects with the highest possible quality diet.

In addition, immediately before they are fed to the lizards, food insects may be placed in a jar or bag with a little calcium-D_3 additive and shaken. Known familiarly as the "shake and bake method," the finely ground powder will adhere to the insects.

Except for field-plankton, all feed insects, even houseflies, are commercially available. It may be your preference to avail yourself regularly of the various commercial sources. Certainly this is less time consuming than breeding your own insects; however, by breeding your own, you can assure that the highest possible diet is continually fed the insects. Even if you procure the insects commercially, you should begin feeding them the best diet possible.

Field Plankton

Insects straight from the wild—commonly called field plankton—have been able to choose their diet and their nutritional value reflects this. To gather them, go to an insecticide-free yard or field and sweep a suitably meshed field net back and forth through tall grasses or low shrubs. These insects, which have fed on natural native foods, are probably at their pinnacle of health. Fed immediately after collecting, the health and full guts of the insects will greatly benefit your lizards.

Crickets

The gray cricket (*Acheta domesticus*), is readily available from fishing or pet stores. Other cricket species may be hand-collected (if your patience holds out) in small numbers beneath debris in fields, meadows, and open woodlands. All species are ideal lizard fare.

Where to get them. If you use more than 500 crickets a week, purchase them directly from wholesale producers that advertise in fishing or reptile magazines. You will find the prices are quite reasonable when crickets are purchased in multiples of 1,000.

Cricket care. Crickets fed on potatoes are fine for fishing, but you need to offer them a better diet if they are to benefit your lizards. Feed your crickets a good and varied diet of your own making, or one of the nutritious, specifically formulated cricket foods now on the market. Among other foods, fresh carrots, potatoes, broccoli, oranges, squash, sprouts, and chick laying mash, will be readily consumed. All foods offered to your crickets should be sprinkled with calcium/D_3, not so much for the benefit of the insects as for the benefit of the lizards to which the crickets are fed.

While crickets will get much of the moisture requirements from their fruit and vegetables, they will also appreciate a water source. Crickets will drown easily if they are given only a plain, shallow dish of water. Instead, place cotton balls, a sponge, or even pebbles or aquarium gravel in the water dish to give the crickets sufficient purchase to climb back out when they fall in.

Cricket housing. Keep crumpled newspapers, the center tubes from rolls of paper towels, or other such hiding areas in the crickets' cage. We prefer the paper towel tubes as they can be lifted and the requisite number of crickets shaken from inside them into the cage or a transportation jar. This makes handling the fast-moving, agile insects easy.

A tightly covered 20-gallon (75.7 L) long tank will temporarily house 1,000 crickets. A substrate of sawdust, soil, vermiculite, or other such medium should be present. This must be

A male green water dragon is a handsome and alert lizard.

changed often to prevent excessive odor from the insects.

Breeding your own. If you choose to breed your own crickets, this is not difficult. Keep the cricket cage between 76 and 86°F (24–30°C). Place a shallow dish of slightly moistened sand, vermiculite, or even cotton balls on the floor of the cage. The material in this dish will be the laying medium and will need to be kept very slightly moistened throughout the laying, incubation, and hatching process. Adult crickets are easily sexed. Females will have three "tubes" (the central one being the egg-depositing ovipositor) projecting from the rear of their bodies. Males lack the central ovipositor. The ovipositor is inserted into the laying medium and the eggs expelled. The eggs will hatch in from 8 to 20 days, the duration being determined by cricket species and tank temperature. Nutritious food should always be available to the baby cricket.

Uses for the hatchlings. Newly hatched crickets are ideal for hatchling anoles and other small species of lizards, or the babies of most larger species. Pinhead-sized crickets may be the largest morsel that the hatchlings of some of the smallest anoles can initially handle.

Grasshoppers/Locusts

Grasshoppers and locusts (*Locusta* sp. and *Shistocerca* sp. in part) are widely used as reptile and amphibian foods in European and Asian countries, and are commercially available there. In the United States, you'll have to breed them or collect them in the field. A field net will help you gather these fast-moving insects.

Do not feed lubber grasshoppers, those brightly colored, fat grasshoppers found in the southern states; the nymphs can be fatal if eaten by your specimens. The tan and buff adults seem to be less toxic but their use as a food item is chancy.

Waxworms

The waxworm (*Galleria* sp.) is really a caterpillar, the larval stage of the wax moth found in neglected beehives. They are frequently used as fish bait, and are available from bait stores. Some pet shops sell waxworms. If you need large quantities, check the ads in any reptile and amphibian magazine for wholesale distributors.

Waxworm tips. If you buy quantities of waxworms, you will need to feed them. Chick laying mash, wheat germ, honey, and yeast mixed into a syrupy paste will serve adequately as the diet for these insects; keep the unused portion in your refrigerator.

Giant Mealworms

Giant mealworms, *Zoophobas* sp., are the larvae of a South American beetle. They are rather new in the herpetocultural trade and have proven to be a great food source for many insectivorous herps. Although they are available in many areas of the United States, their future availability may be restricted by the Department of Agriculture; however, they are easy to maintain and breed.

Keeping your own. *Zoophobas* can be kept in quantity in shallow plastic trays containing an inch or so of sawdust. They can be fed a diet of chicken starting mash, bran, leafy vegetables, and apples.

Breeding your own. To do this, set up a series of small containers, such as film containers, each of which contains some sawdust, bran, or oats. Add one mealworm to each container. This sort of close quarters will induce pupation. You can put the smaller containers together in a larger box, simply to make them easier to handle. The worms will pupate and metamorphose into a 1¼-inch-long (37 cm) black beetle. Put the beetles together in a plastic bucket with a sawdust substrate. Add cracked limbs and twigs for egg laying (the female beetles deposit their eggs in the crevices in the limbs). The beetles and their larvae can be fed vegetables, fruits, and oats and bran, added to the adult bucket house. The mealworms will obtain all of their moisture requirements from the fresh vegetables and fruit.

Multiple colonies. You can keep several colonies rotating to be sure that you have all sizes of the larvae to offer your lizards. Although giant mealworms seem to be more easily digested by the lizards than common mealworms, neither species should be fed in excess.

Mealworms

A common food item favored by neophyte reptile and amphibian keepers, mealworms (*Tenebrio molitor*) should actually be fed sparingly, due to the large amounts of chitin they contain. They are easily kept and bred at normal room temperatures in plastic receptacles containing a 2- to 3-inch (5.1–7.6 cm) layer of bran for food and a potato or apple for their moisture requirements. It takes no special measures to breed these insects.

Butterworms

Once readily available, the South American butterworm, *Chilecomadia* sp., is becoming increasingly difficult to find. In appearance these larvae are very much like a corpulent, low-chitin mealworm. They appear to provide good nutrition and most lizards eat them readily. They feed on cereal or bran.

Roaches

Although roaches can be bred, it is nearly as easy to collect them as needed. Roaches are present over much of the world. The size of the roach should be tailored to the size of the animal being fed. A meal of several small roaches is more easily digested than one or two large roaches.

Termites

These little insects are an ideal food for baby anoles, cone-heads, and casque-heads, and even the babies of the smaller basilisks. Collect fresh as necessary. Should you decide to hold "extras" over, they may be kept in some of the slightly dampened wood in which you originally found them. Termites are most easily collected during the damp weather of spring and summer. They are among the best foods for small lizards.

Houseflies

Although these may be collected as needed (weather permitting) in commercial flytraps or bred, genetically engineered flightless houseflies have recently become available. Flies, and their larvae (maggots), are relished by many anoles, by cone-headed lizards, and by babies of many other forms discussed in this book.

Flies can be bred in tightly covered, wide-mouthed gallon jars. The larvae (maggots) will thrive in putrefying meat, overripe fruit and vegetables, or other such medium.

The simplest method of introducing the adult flies to the cage is to place the entire jar inside the cage before opening it. By using this method, fewer will escape. The maggots can be removed by hand or with forceps and placed in a shallow dish.

Mice

Mice are easily bred. A single male to two or three females in a rodent breeding cage will produce a rather steady supply of babies that can be fed to the lizards that will accept them. Mice can be fed in small numbers to basilisks, water dragons, and sail-tailed lizards. Some of the very large anole species, such as the Jamaican giant and the knight anoles, may also accept an occasional pinky.

We suggest that you use aspen or pine shavings for the bedding for the mice. Feed your mice either a "lab chow" diet that is specifically formulated for them, or a healthy mixture of seeds and vegetables. Fresh water must be present at all times.

Our tip: DO NOT use cedar bedding for your mice; the phenols contained in cedar can be harmful to both reptiles and amphibians.

Honey-fruit Mix

Anoles, and to a lesser degree, basilisks and dragons, will also lap at a honey-fruit mixture. Below is the formula we use:

⅓ jar of mixed fruit or apricot strained baby food
⅓ jar of strained papaya baby food
1 teaspoon honey

⅓ eyedropper of Avitron liquid bird vitamins
½ teaspoon of Osteoform powdered vitamins
Add water to attain desired consistency
A small quantity of bee pollen can be added if it is available.

Watering

Ascertaining that your anoles, or other persistently arboreal lizard species, drink enough water may be even more difficult than monitoring their food intake. The basilisks and water dragons should pose no problems in this respect. In the wild, anoles drink pendulous droplets that either fall or condense on leaves, twigs, or even their own bodies. Simply put, anoles often (but not always) have difficulty recognizing quietly standing water as a drinking source.

When outdoors. Our step-in cages are gently sprinkled twice daily for a period of several minutes. Thirsty lizards drink copiously at these times.

Occasionally we use a second, almost as effective method of watering the lizards in these large cages. Several pinhead-sized holes are placed in the bottom of a large plastic bucket. The bucket is then filled with tap water and placed atop the cage above the tree. The water drips slowly from the pin-holes, providing the lizards with a drinking source for a quarter hour or so. Within moments after the drip system is operational, anoles and cone-headed lizards gather to drink in the uppermost foliage and, in cages housing larger basilisks, the lizards station themselves in a splash zone on a sturdy inner limb or on the cage floor. The shade-loving casque-headed lizards drink the water as it trickles through the lower foliage and along the trunks and limbs.

Cages of wood and wire construction lend themselves well to these outside watering techniques. Once hitting the floor of the cage, the water merely runs out and away. The immediate runoff prevents the formation of standing water that would be detrimental to the health of your lizard. The bucket method, using a smaller bucket, can also be used in indoor terraria. Since most indoor terraria have watertight bottoms and sides, the water accumulated in the water receptacle will need to be removed daily.

A third method can be easily adapted to either indoor or outdoor terraria/cages. As mentioned, neither anoles nor most other arboreal reptiles readily recognize quietly standing water as a drinking source. However, if that same water is roiled, as with a bubbling aquarium airstone, it is often readily recognizable. This is especially so if the water receptacles are elevated away from the bottom of the lizard's cage.

For swimmers. Water dragons and basilisks enjoy large water receptacles into which they may drop, sit, or submerge. All six of the species in these two genera are often associated with water-edge habitats in the wild. Large water/swimming containers are thus extensively used by these lizards.

Use an airstone to move the water in a drinking dish.

"Naturalistic ponds" can be built, but even when filtered, they are usually difficult to keep clean. As unaesthetic as they may be, plastic kitty-litter pans or dish-washing tubs are among the most functional, inexpensive, and readily available water containers for larger lizards. Tubs of neutral colors do not contrast as sharply and adversely with their surroundings as those hued in bright blues, yellows, or reds. Should you choose to do so, a framework of rocks or horizontal limbs may be built to at least partially hide the outline of these containers.

Your Lizards' Health

Once you have selected a healthy-looking lizard as your pet, brought it home, placed it in your caging setup, and watched it feed and drink readily, do not think the battle is over. You need to watch over your pet and observe its behavior for clues to possible illness. Whether large or small, you lizard deserves good treatment when it is ill.

Hydration Chambers

The uses and benefits of "hydration chambers" have long been appreciated by zoos and other public institutions. They are only now coming into general use by private herpetoculturists and hobbyists. The term "hydration chamber" is merely a highfalutin' way of saying "rain chamber." But there is nothing highfalutin' about the rain chamber's value to the herpetoculturist. These receptacles can make the difference between life and death for dehydrated lizards, and can be used,

at least partially, to replicate rainy seasons as well. As we have discussed, the seasonal rains often play an important function in the reproductive cycling of many lizards. A week or so of daily mistings in a hydration chamber will often have the same stimulating effect as natural rains.

Making your own: A hydration chamber can be constructed of wire mesh over a wood frame, or of an aquarium equipped with a circulating water pump and a screen or perforated plexiglass top. If you are fortunate enough to live in a benign climate where the cage can be placed outdoors, a mist nozzle can be placed on the end of a hose, affixed over the cage, and fresh water run through this for an hour or more a day. Neither chlorinates nor chloramines will unduly affect your lizards.

If indoors, the cage can be placed on top, or inside of a properly drained utility tub and the fresh water system used. It is imperative that the drain system be adequate and kept free of debris if this system is used indoors. A secondary (backup) drain (just in case. . .) might do much to guarantee your peace of mind.

In contained systems, the circulation pump can force water from the tank itself through a small diameter PVC pipe into which a series of lateral holes has been drilled, or merely brought up to the top of the tank and allowed to drip through the screen or perforated plexiglass. It is imperative that the water in self-contained systems be kept immaculately clean.

Why use a chamber? The use of these (or similar) units can do much to help moisture-starved herptiles recu-

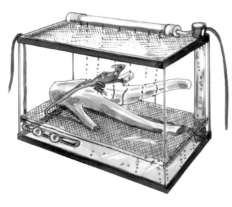

Use the hydration chamber to re-hydrate a newly acquired lizard.

perate. Those that will most benefit from such a structure are the rain-forest species that are freighted long distances to reach the pet markets of America, Asia, Europe and other countries. Newly received anoles, casque- and cone-headed lizards, as well as baby basilisks, water dragons and sail-tailed lizards are all prime candidates for hydration chamber treatment.

Green anoles assume their brightest color when placidly basking in the warm rays of a late afternoon sun.

The Veterinarian

Making a decision of whether a $1.99 green or brown anole should be taken to a veterinarian when it is ailing is always difficult. Adding to the indecision is the sad fact that, once a lizard as small as an anole begins to *look* sick, it is often too ill to save, no matter how heroic the veterinary intervention. Perhaps because they are larger and more costly, lizard keepers seem to have less problem seeking medical help for basilisks, water dragons, and sail-tailed dragons when necessary.

Many of us ask whether we shouldn't just "let nature take her course" and then replace the lizard if it dies. That is really a personal decision, but we feel that the lizard is deserving of whatever help we are able to offer. Once the lizard has been removed from the wild, we, not Mother Nature, are in charge of its well-being—its destiny. And, even if you are unable to save that particular lizard, after seeing it your veterinarian may be able to offer suggestions that will prevent a replay of the scenario with your next lizard.

Finding a qualified reptile veterinarian is not always an easy task. Once a stepchild of the veterinary field, the veterinary care of reptiles and amphibians is now a specialized discipline. An association of qualified veterinarians provides regular interchanges of ideas, technology, and accepted practices to among the member specialists. Veterinarians do not necessarily have to be members to be competent in the care of reptiles and amphibians, but this professional association does help them remain abreast of new technology.

Find a Veterinarian Early

By the time anoles, basilisks, and water dragons (or any other lizards, for that matter) manifest external signs of ailments, they are usually very ill. Therefore, we strongly suggest that you locate a reptile veterinarian before you need one and discuss the costs of office visits and medications in advance. It neither costs less nor takes less time for a veterinarian to look at and treat an anole than it does to perform the same service on a cat or dog. As a matter of fact, because of the small size of the anole and the toxicity of some medications to reptiles, treating the anole will necessarily be more exacting.

Nutrition-related Maladies

Metabolic Bone Disease (MBD)

Symptoms. MBD is typified by the softening of the bones. Pliability in the lower jawbones, kinking of the tail, limb swelling, and lack of rigidity in the leg bones are all diagnostic signs.

This is perhaps the most common insidious and pervasive disease that you (and your lizard) are apt to encounter. MBD is known by several other names as well, among them *decalcification*, *demineralization*, and *fibrous osteodystrophy*. Improper metabolization of calcium, or insufficient quantities of calcium available, causes this disease.

Since this is a disease encountered time and again, let's take a more extensive look at the problem, and discuss how to avoid it.

Problem areas. Watching and correcting five potential problem areas will help you stave off MBD:

1. Provide unfiltered natural sunlight (best) or full-spectrum lighting (distant second).

2. Provide vitamin D_3.

3. Provide calcium.

4. The dietary calcium:phosphorus ratio *must* be a minimum of 2:1 (3:1 is even better).

5. Do not feed omnivorous lizards plant materials containing oxalic acid (a calcium binder; among others, spinach and *Oxalis*, or wood sorrel, are such plants).

Here are the reasons for the above five points:

Ultraviolet rays (UV-B), from natural sunlight, or from artificial sources, help reptiles synthesize vitamin D_3 in the skin. Without the presence of D_3, calcium, even when amply provided, cannot be properly metabolized. Sadly, the vast majority of most bulbs now on the market do not provide a great deal of UV. This includes many that are currently billed as full-spectrum. No, or reduced, UV-B equals no, or reduced, D_3 synthesization; thus, an artificial source of D_3 must be provided. Vitamin D_3 *must* be present for the reptile to metabolize calcium.

The presence of high levels of phosphorus will offset the beneficial aspects of calcium; therefore, the overall diet, including supplements, should provide a minimum of two times more calcium than phosphorus (3:1 in favor of calcium would probably be better).

The oxalic acid contained naturally in plants such as spinach and wood

sorrel can be at least as detrimental as the phosphorus. Oxalic acid binds with the calcium to form calcium oxylate. Calcium so affected is of no benefit whatever and can even cause kidney damage.

Therefore, the seemingly obvious solution, when natural, unfiltered, sunlight is not available, is to provide a proper and well-rounded diet, as well as vitamin D_3, and calcium supplements.

Don't wait! Once MBD is well advanced, veterinary intervention becomes mandatory and may not be effective. Treatment then involves the use of injectable calcium and immediate diet correction. If the jawbones are too weakened, your lizards may have trouble eating and require force-feeding of a calcium-enhanced soft diet. Prevention is certainly better than treatment.

Articular and Visceral Gout

Symptoms. Swelling of, and difficulty in moving, joints; inflammation and hardening of internal organs.

Diet. Although gout does not appear to occur in insect-eating and omnivorous lizards with the same degree of regularity as with improperly fed herbivorous lizards, it is occasionally reported. Gout is most often related to improper hydration but is now recognized as being diet-related, and perhaps temperature-related as well. Certain zoo studies have connected

---

Medical abbreviations
mg —milligram
    (1 mg = 0.001 gram)
kg —kilogram
    (1000 grams; 2.2 pounds)
mcg —microgram
    (1 mcg = 0.000001 gram)
IM —intramuscularly
IP —intraperitoneally
PO —orally

Medications and Dosages

Many lizards, even those that are captive-bred and hatched, may harbor internal parasites. Because of the complexities of identification of endoparasites and the necessity to accurately weigh specimens to be treated and measure purge dosages, the eradication of internal parasites is best left to a qualified reptile veterinarian. These are a few of the recommended medications and dosages, which are usually based on the weight of the animal. These medications and dosages were suggested by Dr. Richard Funk, a reptile veterinarian in southwest Florida.

Amoebas and Trichomonads: **Metronidazole** given orally, 40–50 mg/kg. The treatment is repeated in two weeks.

Dimetridazole can also be used but the dosage is very different. 40–50 mg/kg of Dimetrizadole is administered daily for five days; the treatment is then repeated in two weeks. All treatments with both medications are administered once daily.

Coccidia: Many treatments are available.

The dosages of **sulfadiazine**, **sulfamerazine**, and **sulfamethazine** are identical. Administer 75 mg/kg the first day, then follow up for the next five days with 45 mg/kg.

All treatments orally and once daily.

Sulfadimethoxine is also effective. The initial dosage is 90 mg/kg orally to be followed on the next five days with 45 mg/kg orally.

All dosages are administered once daily.

Trimethoprim-sulfa may also be used; 30 mg/kg should be administered once daily for seven days.

Cestodes (Tapeworms): Several effective treatments are available.

Bunamidine may be administered orally at a dosage of 50 mg/kg.

A second treatment occurs in 14 days.

Niclosamide; given orally, at a dosage of 150 mg/kg, is also effective.

A second treatment is given in two weeks.

Praziquantel may be administered either orally or intramuscularly. The dosage is 5–8 mg/kg and is to be repeated in 14 days.

Trematodes (Flukes): **Praziquantel** at 8 mg/kg may be administered either orally or intramuscularly.

The treatment is repeated in two weeks.

Some veterinarians prefer the oral administration.

Nematodes (Roundworms): Several effective treatments are available.

Levamisole, an injectable intraperitoneal treatment, should be administered at a dosage of 10 mg/kg and the treatment repeated in two weeks.

Ivermectin, injected intramuscularly in a dosage of 200 mcg/kg is effective. The treatment is to be repeated in two weeks. Some veterinarians prefer oral administration of this medication. Ivermectin can be toxic to certain taxa.

Thiabendazole and **Fenbendazole** have similar dosages. Both are administered orally at 50–100 mg/kg and repeated in 14 days.

Mebendazole is administered orally at a dosage of 20–25 mg/kg and repeated in 14 days.

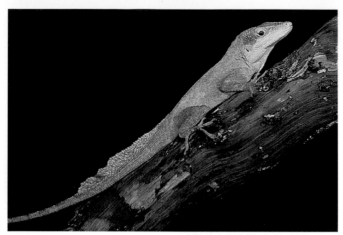

Anolis ferreus, *the sail-tailed anole from Marie Gallante, has now been found on a few occasions in southern Florida. It is not yet known whether this is an established alien species in the state.*

Gastrointestinal Impactions

Causes. Impactions (blockages) can and do occur in lizards. At times, insufficient gut moisture may cause food items to dry, accumulate, and lead to impaction. Properly hydrated lizards and lizards fed a proper diet are less likely to incur food impactions than lizards kept and fed suboptimally.

Impactions can also be caused by lizards (purposely or accidentally) ingesting stones, dirt, or gravel, dried corncobs, or other such substrate.

Treatment. Each impaction must be assessed individually. Exercise, and especially swimming, may help your lizard to excrete the impaction normally and without intervention; however, some impactions may require mechanical softening or surgery. Consult your veterinarian.

Parasites

Many wild-collected basilisks, and *most* wild-collected water dragons and sail-tailed dragons, bear heavy (and potentially lethal) loads of endoparasites. Unless eradicated, parasites will often debilitate not only the lizard in question but will infect all other lizards in the terrarium. It is a good idea to have fecal smears and floats performed whenever you acquire a new lizard of any of the highly aquatic species (arboreal lizards tend to bear fewer parasites). Isolate new arrivals from established specimens until good health has been ascertained, or until all necessary regimens of medication and purging have been completed.

Endo- (Internal) Parasites

Symptoms. When lizards are stressed by the trauma of capture, shipping, and handling, endoparasites often proliferate, at times to lethal proportions. Be especially vigilant of the weight and overall appearance of newly received, wild-collected, partially aquatic species. Failure to eat, failure

gout to temperatures that are not high enough to allow proper and full metabolism of food items. Still, gout seems most commonly reported in herbivorous lizards that are fed moderate to large quantities of animal protein.

Gout has been reported in water dragons, sail-tailed lizards, and basilisks that are fed mostly or entirely on mice. This again points out how necessary "natural" and varied diets are. In the wild, both water dragons and sail-tailed lizards eat a fair amount of vegetation and a preponderance of insects. Basilisks seem basically insectivorous, although we have had some that have eagerly lapped up honey-fruit mixture and eaten the petals of fresh blossoms. It is probable that only small numbers of nestling mammals and birds are consumed by any of these lizards in the wild.

We have again allowed ease of availability, rather than common sense, to govern our feeding. No matter how we strive, it will never be possible for us to feed our captive lizards a fraction of the dietary diversity they would get in the wild—but at least we can try.

to gain weight, or weight loss, may indicate burgeoning parasite loads. Internal parasites may also cause odorous stools and diarrhea. Any of these symptoms, either singly or in combination, can quickly have devastating results. Consult your veterinarian for diagnosis and treatment.

As we realize that in many parts of the world reptile veterinarians are either difficult to find or actually nonexistent, some medications and dosages commonly used in treating endoparasites in reptiles are listed on page 43. This information is not intended to promote home use, but rather to help a non-specialist when you consult him or her with your problems.

Ectoparasites (Ticks and Mites)

Ticks are often found on wild-caught specimens. They are easily removed by first daubing their body with rubbing alcohol, then, after a few minutes, gently but steadily pulling them free with your fingers or with forceps. Since you want to remove them with mouthparts intact, do not jerk them sharply. Once they have been removed, you can daub the puncture made by the mouthparts with rubbing alcohol.

Mites are less of a problem on lizards than on snakes, but they are occasionally encountered. Mites can be seen as tiny pepper-grain-sized black specks moving animatedly about on both the lizard and its terrarium. Mites especially favor the wrinkles around eyelids, armpits, and femoral area.

Avoid problems. If you keep lizards in naturalistic terraria (heavily planted terraria with soil, logs, and rocks), it is especially important that you quarantine all lizards and eradicate mites *before* putting the lizards in their permanent terrarium. Mites will be next to impossible to eradicate if any enter the naturalistic setup. Should you be

unfortunate enough to have mites become established in the naturalistic terrarium, several exposures to a No-Pest strip (or its generic equivalent) may help to reduce them. Remove the lizards and treat them in a separate enclosure while you are treating their vivarium. If treatments at nine-day intervals do not eliminate the mites from the elaborate terraria, disassemble the tank and replace the substrate, plantings, and perches with new, mite-free accessories.

To treat lizards in a small terraria, suspend a small piece of a No-Pest strip (½ inch × 1 inch [12.7–25 mm]) in a wire receptacle (so the lizards cannot come in direct contact with it) from the top of the terrarium for three days. The permanent water source should be removed during treatment. Unlike snakes, which can easily subsist for the three-day treatment period without water, your lizards may be unable to do so. Therefore, we suggest that you water them for at least an hour a day. If you have anoles or cone-headed lizards that you water by misting, do this in a separate tank. Do not wet the No-Pest strip. After three days, remove the No-Pest, and replace the water container; repeat the process nine days later.

Again—be *absolutely certain* to quarantine and treat all lizards for mites (or any other malady for that matter) before putting them in a naturalistic vivarium.

Other treatments include injections of Ivermectin, now being used by many veterinarians to combat mites on snakes. Its toxicity to lizards is largely unknown. The mites die after biting the animals so treated. In dry climates, a desiccant powder called "Dry-Die" can be used effectively. It is available from many reptile dealers and livestock feed stores.

Trichlorfon spray may prove effective on some lizards but it is already known to be fatally toxic to many taxa of geckos. Whether its effects are detrimental to the health of other lizard taxa remains largely unknown.

In all cases, clean and sterilize as much of the cage and cage furniture as possible; five percent Clorox bleach is a good disinfectant. Rinse all items cleaned with bleach thoroughly before reusing them. Repeat as necessary. Mites can hide in the smallest of crevices and it is entirely possible for those that remain behind to reinfest your lizard colony.

Trauma-related Maladies

Nose Injuries

Bloodied and bruised noses are commonly seen in the fast-moving basilisks, water dragons, and sail-tailed lizards. These are often initially caused by abrasion in the collecting/shipping containers, and is often worsened by the frightened lizards repeatedly careening into the sides of their terraria/cages. Neosporin or other such antibiotic ointment may help to soothe and heal the abraded area. Reptile veterinarian, Dr. Frederic L. Frye, has suggested the use of a liquid bandage (such as Newskin) on seriously injured parts.

Left untreated, or if repeatedly reinjured, nose injuries can progress to mouth rot (infectious stomatitis, literally an infection of the stoma or mouth). See comments below.

Infectious Stomatitis (Mouth Rot)

Symptoms. Mouth rot is identifiable by the presence of white cheesy (caseous) material on the gums and teeth of the infected specimen. It is most often seen in the proximity of mouth damage. As with all other problems, prevention is always better than cure; before the mouth rot becomes established, eliminate the cause. Use visual barriers such as paper or

opaque plastic taped onto tank walls to "warn" flighty species about the limits of their cages.

Although this problem is seldom encountered in anoles, casque-headed lizards, or cone-headed lizards, mouth rot is seen in the larger, nose-rubbing species, such as basilisks, water dragons, and sail-tailed lizards. Fortunately, not every case of bruising or other nose damage results in mouth rot, but when nose damage is recurring and/or hygiene somewhat less than acceptable, mouth rot can occur.

Treatment. Bruises and abrasions should be treated as they occur. In many cases, before actual infection has occurred, the simple, periodic, topical application of a good antibiotic (Neosporin, Polysporin, etc.) will usually suffice. If mouth rot has begun, *gently* remove all loose and affixed caseous material with a Betadine-dipped cotton swab. Reswab the infected area with Betadine. Apply an antibiotic cream.

It is very important that the cause of the abrasions/bruising be removed or corrected. In the case of one huge male red-headed basilisk we once had, even taping opaque papers over the glass in his enclosure was not enough to keep him from repeatedly running into the barriers and damaging his snout. It actually became necessary to affix top-to-bottom soft cotton drapes a few inches inside of the back and ends of his cage and to keep the entire front opaque as well.

Note: The flight-reactions of many large active adult lizards are deeply ingrained and difficult to impossible to overcome. You should always keep in mind the possibility that you will not be able to tame such a lizard *before* you make the purchase.

We suggest that whenever possible you acquire captive-bred and hatched specimens, or, should this not be possible, that you at least purchase the smaller (and often more easily tamed) lizards.

Broken Bones

Light-bodied arboreal lizards are well adapted to dropping/falling long distances with no problems whatever. Heavier-bodied, more terrestrial species are less well adapted. In captivity, probably because of artificial environments and diets, broken bones occur with some frequency. Having a heavy piece of cage furniture settle down on top of them can quickly cause a break. In most cases, it is the leg bones that break. In some cases, it may be a break (or a disarticulation) of the spinal vertebrae. Back injuries are particularly serious and can result in partial or full paralysis. In the latter case, euthanasia is recommended. In all cases, even the least serious, veterinary assistance should be immediately sought, and the environment (and, perhaps, diet) changed/adjusted to prevent recurrence. Improper diet will play a part by allowing weakening or demineralizing of bone structure.

Tail Breaks

At last we come to a problem that, although disfiguring, is often not particularly serious. The breaking off (autotomization) of the tail is a predator-avoidance adaptation. Most lizards are capable of such tail loss with little discomfort. Some lizards (perhaps even most, but definitely not all) are capable of tail regeneration. The lizards best adapted for tail autotomization have a weakened area in anywhere from a few to many of the caudal vertebrae. These weakened areas are termed *caudal planes* and are generally in the distal two-thirds of the tail. If the break occurs at one of these areas, regeneration usually begins swiftly. Also, regeneration is most complete when the break occurs at a caudal plane. If the break occurs at a point

other than a caudal plane, regeneration may be minimal or not occur at all. This is especially true if the break is very close to the body. When occurring at a caudal plane, the break is accompanied by very little bleeding. The area of the break needs only to be kept dry and clean until it dries somewhat. If the break occurs at a point other than at a caudal plane, more bleeding may be evident. Even if it is on the distal half of the tail, veterinary intervention is seldom necessary. Again, keep the tip dry and clean until it dries.

If the break is near the body, an area where there are usually no caudal planes and that is more highly vascularized, extensive bleeding requiring cauterization and stitching may occur. Seek the advice and services of your veterinarian if the break looks uncomfortable or is in a particularly fleshy area.

Incomplete or uneven breaks may cause the generation of two or more tails.

Burns

The rather primitive nervous system of a lizard will allow it to come to harm from malfunctioning heating units before the lizard is actually aware of the damage. If all heating equipment in use is regulated and functioning properly, burns seldom occur; however, at some point, malfunctions of regulatory equipment (rheostats/thermostats) may occur, causing your lizards to sustain thermal burns. Inappropriately regulated heat tapes, heating pads, hot rocks, or heating limbs can cause burns to the ventral surfaces of your lizard's body and limbs. The use of these items can also overheat and destroy eggs still in the females' oviducts. Ventral burns may initially appear raw and reddish and may or may not suppurate. As they heal they become rusty-red and either flaky or scabby. Since, with exception of the little casque-headed

Regenerated tails are scaled, and often colored, differently than the original. Anoles, basilisks, and water dragons can all regenerate broken tails. A distal break usually regenerates more completely than an anterior break.

lizards of the genus *Corytophanes*, all of the lizards discussed in this book are heliotherms (species that bask in the sunlight), we strongly suggest that you avoid using ventral heaters. Warmth and illumination are best provided from above for these lizards. Even the little casque-headed lizards, denizens of the shadowy realms of the understory in forested habitats, will thermoregulate in patches of sunlight when necessary, but seem more dependent on the ambient temperatures within their woodland home.

Unshielded overhead bulbs in cages or strong heat lamps positioned too closely above a cage can cause thermal burns to dorsal surfaces of your lizards. Use extreme care when selecting bulb wattage and positioning the lighting unit.

If a burn does occur, immediately correct the malfunctioning implement, adjust the distance between the overhead bulb and the cage top, and treat the lizard's burn with a good quality antibiotic ointment.

Overheating (Hyperthermia)

Overly warm temperatures can be as lethal to reptiles as overly cold ones. We suggest that the terrarium/cage temperatures for all of the lizard species discussed in this book be in the 76 to 82°F (24–28°C) range. Providing a warmer basking area will allow the lizards to regulate their body temperature upwards if they so desire, and by retreating from the basking area they can again cool themselves.

If your terrarium is completely enclosed, a few unexpected minutes of direct sunlight can cause lethal overheating. Be careful where you situate your tank and be aware of the seasonal changes in the position and intensity of the sun's rays.

Initially overheated lizards will gape and actively try to escape their quarters. If cooling does not quickly occur they then become unresponsive and usually undergo a quite considerable change in coloration, even normally dark specimens often becoming a patchy or pasty gray. If they are still alive when found, cool the lizards immediately in a tub or sink of 72 to 76°F (22–24°C) water. If you've begun this in time, your lizards will live, although they may display neurological problems associated with brain damage. Of course, repositioning or shielding the tank is mandatory.

Overcooling (Hypothermia)

Exposure to cold temperatures can cause many of the same reactions as overheating, but, rather than initially becoming overactive, the affected lizards merely lapse into a state of lethargy, and instead of becoming light in color, they often become dark. Hypothermia most often occurs during the winter in northern climes during power outages or when a lizard escapes from its warmed enclosure into unsuitably heated areas. Although cooling is seldom as quickly fatal as overheating, respiratory ailments are not uncommon following prolonged hypothermia. Warm the lizards in a terrarium of suitable temperature—80 to 88°F (26.7–31°C) or by immersing all but their head in a tub of 80 to 88°F (26.7–31°C) water.

Respiratory Ailments

Unless captive conditions remain poor over a fairly long period of time, most of the lizards discussed in this book are rather resistant to respiratory ailments. Badly stressed wild-collected lizards arriving at the establishments of dealers or hobbyists during the winter may have respiratory ailments, however. Power outages that cause a sharp drop in temperature in humid tanks also cause respiratory problems. Continued maintenance of terrarium temperatures below suitable parameters can be another culprit. A number of different bacteria can be involved in respiratory ailments.

Raise the temperature in your terrarium to 87 to 90°F (30.5–32.2°C); do not lower it at night. Have a veterinarian assess the severity of the problem. Isolating the pathogen and determining its sensitivity to specific medications, in case such are needed, is mandatory.

Blister Disease

Although blister disease is not a common malady among anoles, basilisks, water dragons, and allies, it can occur. If forced to remain in contact with a substrate that is too moist or, especially, moist and fouled, or in

If given plenty of cover in a large terrarium, Jamaican giant anoles make excellent terrarium lizards.

fouled water, blisters and pustules can appear on the skin. In all but the most advanced cases, progression of this bacterial (or, rarely, bacterial *and* fungal) disease can be halted by moving the lizards to drier, clean quarters. The blemishes will usually be removed when the lizard next sheds. Shedding sequences are often of increased frequency when blisters (or other skin lesions) are present. In advanced cases, where the lesions reach into body tissues, treatment by a qualified veterinarian must be immediately sought.

Breeding Lizards

Proper conditioning throughout the year, and especially for the few months prior to the breeding season, is of paramount importance if you intend to breed your anole, basilisk, or water dragon. The conditioning process is every bit as important for captives as for wild-ranging specimens. The reproductive cycles of lizards is triggered by conditions that exist long before the actual breeding season. Among these conditions are:

- recovered body weight
- temperature
- rainfall and humidity variations
- photoperiods
- successful brumation or dormancy (if applicable)
- dominance factors, and others, some of which we still don't understand.

Although many of the conditions necessary to breed anoles, basilisks, water dragons, and allied species are similar, there are many slight quirks that must be addressed between groups (sometimes between species).

Feeding. When temperatures cool, the metabolism and bodily functions of lizards slow. When temperatures get too cold, bodily functions cease. Thus, when cool, lizards eat less and take longer to digest what they have eaten. Cut back on both the size of the servings and the frequency with which they are offered while your lizards are being cooled in the winter. Hibernating specimens will not, of course, be fed at all.

Anoles may require feeding only every second or third day and water dragons only once or twice a week. Knowing your lizards and their actions and reactions will help immensely during this period. They will tell you when they are hungry.

Egg retention. If conditions within their cage are not suitable for egg deposition, female lizards may be reluctant to lay their clutch. Altering cage conditions so that they are more favorable may induce the female to lay. Such things as deepening the substrate, or altering its moisture content, may be all that is necessary. Providing a feeling of more security for the female by moving the terrarium to a less heavily trafficked area, or by providing a darkened "cave" in which the female can conceal herself during the nesting sequence may help. If the female is still reluctant to lay, an injection of oxytocin or other such hormone, may be required. In the most extreme cases (when due to a solidified egg retained from an earlier clutch, or other physical problem, the female is *unable* to lay), surgical removal of the eggs may become necessary. Consult your veterinarian.

Changes in the shells. Eggs that are viable may discolor somewhat during incubation, but almost never develop "slime," mold, or fungus on their shells. Viable eggs of many lizards that produce parchment-shelled eggs increase noticeably in size during incubation. This size increase allows for the development of the embryo within the shell. Developing eggs may dimple or bulge. This is normal, even with entirely suitable incubating moisture and humidity. However, a noticeable collapse of the shell indicates insufficient moisture in the incubation medium and insufficient relative humidity. If the collapse is noticed quickly enough and the moisture and humidity is raised, the eggs will often continue to develop and hatch perfectly healthy babies.

Age. Both size and age combine to determine a lizard's sexual maturity. Since size is inexorably tied to both the diet and the feeding habits of a lizard, it is very much a variable; however, in general, if properly fed and otherwise cared for, some of the smaller anoles can attain sexual maturity the summer following their hatching. In our limited experience, cone-headed lizards must be at least 18 months old to breed. Many of the larger basilisks and dragons do not attain sexual maturity until they are 30 months of age or older. This is especially true of the brown water dragon, which virtually ceases to grow during its lengthy periods of winter dormancy. Examples of this species may not reproduce until during their fourth year of life.

Breeding Anoles

Cycling

With the exception of the green anole, which ranges as far northward in the United States as North Carolina and Oklahoma, anoles are a subtropical and tropical group of lizards. It is probable that, among the anoles, it is only the more northerly populations of the green anole that have a period of winter dormancy sufficiently long to be thought of as brumation or hibernation. Certainly other nonequatorial species of anoles are affected by the lowered temperatures and humidity and the shorter hours of daylight during the months of winter. Equatorial anole species are affected by seasonal changes in rainfall, thus ambient humidity.

Neither cool, nor dry conditions, are the best for egg deposition and incubation, so during the cooler, shorter, and drier days of the year, anoles are comparatively at ease. During this nonreproductive time, males are not quite so agonistic, and both males and females spend more time simply eating and resting (or in periods of dormancy during particularly inclement weather conditions). During this period of relative benevolence and quiescence, wounds are healed, fat reserves are rebuilt, and the lizards—both males and females—prepare for another season of breeding.

Despite the lack of breeding activity, this period of inactivity is *very* important to the breeding cycle of an anole; its biological clock is reset, and primed responses are lying in wait.

Onset of breeding season. With the lengthening days of summer, the breeding season of anoles begins in earnest. The days of lethargy are over. The increasing photoperiod induces gonadal recrudescence and, in turn, an increasing hormonal flow. Males begin to again determinedly defend territories. Bobbing bodies and flaring dewlaps are evident. The displays are used to both dissuade nearby competing males from indulging in territory invasion and to entice nearby females, also made receptive by the changing seasons, to visit. Entwined anole bodies are soon followed by females seeking suitable egg deposition sites, and, since many females in a given area nest almost simultaneously, a month and a half later, by myriad baby anoles.

Because they are so common and so inexpensive, little attention is given by herpetoculturists to most anoles. This is especially true of the green and the brown anoles, both of which are supplied to pet stores as snake food at least as often as for pets.

Because they are common and rather easily bred in captivity, we strongly urge beginning herpetoculturists to hone their skills on anoles. Breed them, raise them, enjoy them.

Copulation usually occurs in the spring of the year. Anoles may copulate, or at least display, throughout the warm months of the year. This pair of Jamaican giant anoles was breeding on the trunk of a shade tree in Lee County, Florida.

Breeding in Captivity

To breed even the most common species of anoles in captivity, you will need to replicate, to some degree, the seasonal changes described above.

Temperature and lighting. Here in Florida, in our outside cages, we merely let nature take its course. Since even the bottoms of these cages are above the temperature-moderating level of the ground, on extremely cool evenings we provide sufficient heat to keep the cages at 42 to 48°F (5.6–8.9°C) for the green and brown anoles and about 10 degrees warmer for tropical species. Daytime temperatures are also variable, but usually between 63 and 80°F (17–26.7°C). Sunshine usually prevails during the winter months in Florida, offering the anoles extended opportu-

nities to thermoregulate. The natural photoperiod always prevails.

If an attempt is made to keep indoor lizards at these same low temperatures, the anoles often develop respiratory ailments (see previous chapter). This is just one more indicator that quasi-natural conditions are better than entirely artificial ones; however, anoles kept indoors are not difficult to cycle reproductively. We suggest that the low nighttime temperatures to which your lizards are subjected be warmer. Keeping indoor cages warm would be less of a problem. Suggested winter lows would be 58 to 65°F (14–18°C) for green anoles of northern origin, and 62 to 68°F (16.7–20°C) degrees for those of southern origin and for tropical anole species. The normal daytime temperatures, 83 to 88°F (28–31°C), should be provided. It is important that either an artificially lessened or entirely natural photoperiod be maintained during the winter months. If the anole terrarium is in an often used room, the terrarium should be draped with a darkening cloth when the room lighting is on in the evening.

Photoperiod. A breach of photoperiod on one or two occasions may make no difference, but if it happens regularly it may negate other efforts you are making to sequence the breeding cycle. Photoperiod is *very* important. During the cooling and lessening of photoperiod, we also reduce humidity. The balancing act you maintain here is critical. Reduced cage humidity will mean that the anoles will need to drink more frequently. And of course, since most anoles are watered by cage misting—well, you get the picture.

During most of the year, we mist the anoles at least twice daily, besides allowing access to all natural showers. During the winter we reduce the mistings to once daily (none on the occasional rainy winter day) but activate elevated water dishes with water roiled by aquarium air stones. Fortunately, Florida's winter humidity is usually considerably lower than summer humidity, so Mother Nature provides us a helping hand.

The winter regimen should be maintained for from 60 to 75 days.

In the early spring we begin allowing nighttime temperatures to increase, upping them by four or five degrees a week for the first two weeks, and bringing them all the way up to the summer norm on the third week. We simultaneously lengthen photoperiod in indoor setups and increase humidity in both indoor and outdoor cages. Soon every anole in the cages is displaying and breeding and when the anoles have been properly conditioned and have good body weight, the breeding season may last well into the summer months.

When properly cycled, brown water dragons can be bred in captivity. Like the babies of many animals, hatchling brown water dragons have a shortened snout and proportionately large head.

Nesting/Egg Laying

The females of many of the smaller species of anoles lay only a single egg at a time, at biweekly intervals. Courtship, but not necessarily breeding, occurs prior to each deposition. Little attempt is made by the females to construct a structured nest. Rather, they are basically "egg scatterers," and often just lay the egg on top of leaf-covered moist mulch, in a hollow beneath a tuft of grass, under, or against, the moisture-retaining edge of a fallen limb or piece of debris. More rarely they may scratch out a simple, shallow nest that barely covers the egg. At times eggs may be laid in plain sight and left. At other times the female may attempt to scratch debris on top of the egg, or nudge and tamp the egg with her nose until it is more securely hidden in leaves or grass. Some of the larger anoles do dig nests with at least a little more integrity. These anoles, too, lay several clutches a year.

With such cursory nest preparation, it is small wonder that the anoles have evolved to deposit their eggs during the warmest and most humid weather, when climatic and environmental conditions are most favorable to incubation.

Female anoles will lay their eggs atop the soil and then nose the egg into shelter under a bit of leaf.

HOW-TO:
Hibernating the Brown Water Dragon

A refrigerator with an altered thermostat can be used to hibernate your lizards.

The term *brumation* is now often used in place of *hibernation* when reptiles are being discussed; actually, the two terms are somewhat interchangeable.

When NOT to Hibernate the Lizards

To cycle reproductively, the brown water dragon seems to require a period of full hibernation. Readying these lizards for this is somewhat complex. First, be aware that unless your brown water dragons are in top condition they should *not* be hibernated. A long winter dormancy is both physically and physiologically stressful for even the healthiest of lizards. In nature, many lizards that look to be in fine condition when they enter hibernation, succumb during that period.

Hibernation under captive conditions is no less stressful for a lizard, and may actually be more difficult.

Because hibernation can be fraught with problems, even experienced herpetoculturists seldom subject their reptiles to a lengthy period of complete dormancy unless it is absolutely necessary; therefore, it is suggested that, unless you actually are cycling your brown water dragons for breeding, they not be hibernated.

We also suggest that hatchling specimens not be hibernated during their first winter and that prior to hibernating *any*

specimen of *any* age, you assure that the lizards are heavy-bodied, healthy, and endoparasite-free.

It is mandatory that the guts of the lizards you intend to hibernate be free from all food materials prior to dormancy. Digestion shuts down with the cold temperatures necessary for hibernation, and any food left in the gut would putrefy, and cause sickness or death. It is equally important that the lizard(s) be adequately hydrated. Keep water available throughout the following sequence:

Technique

• Begin lowering night temperatures and cutting back on feeding two weeks prior to hibernation.
• Hold lowered night temperatures and discontinue feeding ten days prior to hibernation.
• Be sure photoperiods are also reduced (maximum of ten hours of daylight).

• Begin lowering day temperatures slightly, four days prior to hibernation.
• Again assess the health of the lizards the day prior to placing them in hibernation.

Hobbyists in northern climes may choose to merely move the entire terrarium/cage to an unused room, and letting the room temperature drop into the the mid- to high 50s°F (11.7–15°C). The same can be accomplished with greenhouse setups in temperate areas.

In southern Florida, where winter temperatures do not stay sufficiently low for a long enough period, it was necessary for us to make a hibernaculum out of an old refrigerator. We had a refrigerator repairman put a responsive and easily adjustable temperature control switch in line (bypassing the built-in control). Then we preadjusted the refrigerator temperature to 57°F (13.9°C).

Note: Remember that refrigerators are quite efficient at removing moisture from items stored in them. You must carefully monitor the specimens being hibernated in refrigerators to ascertain that they do not become dehydrated.

Facilitating Artificial Hibernation

To facilitate artificial (out of terrarium) hibernation, we placed the brown water dragons, individually, or in twos, in plastic shoeboxes that contained an ample amount of fresh, *barely moistened* sphagnum moss. If the moss is too wet, the lizards can develop blister disease (see page 49). The shoeboxes were then placed in the refrigerator. The lizards were

Reduce room temperature to 55°F to hibernate all the lizards in a room.

roused (approximately) biweekly and allowed to drink, then placed back in hibernation. We chose to use a 60-day overall hibernating period, and elected to use the months of December and January. Thus, natural photoperiods were still diminishing when the lizards entered hibernation, and were on the increase when the lizards were removed.

Upon removal from hibernation, the brown water dragons were returned immediately to a fully warmed and active status. They would often not feed for a day or two, but were soon back to normal activity status—feeding *and* breeding.

Incubation

Anole eggs are durable and easily hatched. Eggs deposited by captive anoles should be removed from the cage for incubation. Do not rotate the eggs on their horizontal axes when you move them. We use margarine containers or deli cups for egg receptacles. A few pinholes are made in the sides of the cup and the cups are covered after the eggs are in place inside. About a dozen eggs may be placed in each cup; the eggs are neither in contact with each other nor the cup sides. The incubation medium can be slightly moistened perlite, vermiculite, sphagnum moss, sand, or sterile potting soil (soils with preadded fertilizers must be avoided). Sphagnum moss is the medium we prefer and use a very unscientific method of preparing it. Whether the moss has been dry packed (such as the kind purchased from nurseries), or is fresh and alive, we wet it thoroughly by soaking it in warm water for a half hour or so. We then empty the water, gather the moss into a ball, and squeeze as much water from it as we can. We then let it sit a while and squeeze it again, even harder. The moss *must* be only barely moist when the eggs are placed in it. Also, because they are lightweight and easy to work with, we prefer perlite or vermiculite over sand or soil. If "slightly moistened" is just a little too vague, we can be a little more exacting about the preparation of perlite and vermiculite as an incubation medium than we could about the sphagnum. To prepare both the perlite and vermiculite, we use a ratio of about 1:10, water:perlite/vermiculite by volume. Suggested incubation temperature is between 82 and 86°F (27.8–30°C); this is "room temperature" in Florida. At these temperatures, the eggs of green, brown, and many other small anoles will hatch in from 32 to 46 days. A few days longer is usually required for the eggs of the larger species such as the knight and the Jamaican giant anoles.

Types of incubators. We use three kinds. One, the commercially available Hov-a-bator, is usually available in feed stores. The other two are easily constructed. The first of these is also the least expensive and is fairly reliable. The materials needed are:

- an aquarium
- a solid top for the aquarium (a sheet of glass, or even plastic wrap will do)
- a thermostatically controlled submersible aquarium heater
- two bricks
- a plastic shoebox

Put the aquarium on a stand in a convenient, yet dark and out-of-the-way spot, near an electrical outlet. Put about 3 inches (7.6 cm) of water (enough to cover the heater) in the tank. Most submersible heaters come with a pair of suction cups to hold them in place. Affix the heater to the bottom glass of the tank. Turn the heater on and adjust it to hold the water temperature at about 84°F (28.9°C). *Gently* put the two bricks, largest flat side down, in the tank. Place the shoebox on top of the bricks. Make absolutely certain that the shoebox rests securely and will not tip. Place the cups holding the eggs inside the shoebox. The shoebox does not need to be covered, but the egg-holding cups do. Place the top on the aquarium. Evaporation and condensation will keep the relative humidity in the closed tank at close to 100 percent. You might wish to adjust the top slightly to lessen humidity slightly, but not so much that the temperature will vary dramatically (a degree or two variation in either direction will not harm the eggs; more than that might).

The second type of incubator is a dry form, not too dissimilar to the Hov-a-bator. It may be a little less expensive, but unless you enjoy building things, we'd recommend the Hov-a-bator.

To build your own incubator. You will need:

- a hefty styrofoam box with a lid
- a heat tape
- a wafer thermostat
- an indicator light
- a thermometer
- a wire rack
- a plastic shoebox

The heat tape, of course, is wired to the thermostat and placed in the bottom of the styro box. This must be done in such a way that two coils of the tape do not overlap or touch. The thermostat and the indicator light are affixed to the lid (or the upper side) of the styrofoam box and wired onto the heat tape. The tape is then plugged in and the temperature properly adjusted (82 to 86°F [27.8–30°C]). It may take a day or more of periodic adjustments to assure the continued accuracy of the temperature you need. The wire rack is affixed a couple of inches above the heat tape. The plastic shoebox sits securely on the wire rack.

Provided the eggs are fertile, the incubation should now be rather uneventful. Hatchling anoles of the smaller forms are extremely small. They will require fruit flies, termites, pinhead crickets and the tiniest field plankton for not only their first meal, but for several weeks. Hatchling anoles of larger species will willingly accept correspondingly larger food insects.

Breeding Cone-headed and Casque-headed Lizards

Very little is yet known with certainty about the reproductive biology of these basilisk relatives. Of the several species in these two genera, it is the smooth cone-head, *Laemanctus longipes*, which is most commonly bred in captivity. A few zoos and even fewer private hobbyists have succeeded. Cycling methods used for the tropical anoles have succeeded with these lizards. Of the four breedings at our facility, three clutches numbered three eggs each and one numbered four. Up to five eggs in a

Captive bred hatchling green water dragons (top) and green basilisks (center) are offered with increasing frequency.

The outline of the developing eggs can be seen in this female Basiliscus vittatus.

single clutch have been reported. The species multi-clutches.

The nests prepared were all only slight depressions and all were constructed amidst the fibrous roots of a small tree only a few inches from the trunk. In one case, after the deposition, the female nudged the eggs into a more compact grouping with her nose and then haphazardly covered them. At 82 to 86°F (27.8–30°C), incubation lasted from 59 to 68 days. The hatchlings, somewhat paler than the adults, were very slender and mostly tail. The snout-vent length was about 1.75 inches (44 mm) and the tail somewhat more than three times that length. The babies proved delicate. They were reluctant feeders on anything but the smallest of insects, and preferred active baby crickets and grasshoppers over slower-moving insect types. The hatchling *Laemanctus* were also very prone to dehydration, and in the outdoor cages required misting three or four times daily. Once growth began, they seemed hardier, but continued to be very subject to dehydration.

Although we have kept casque-headed lizards for years, we have never successfully bred them. As a matter of fact, we have never seen any indications of courtship; nor have we been able to find records indicating that any of the casque-headed lizards have been bred elsewhere in America. European hobbyists claim that between five and eleven eggs are produced by adult females but have provided no additional information.

Breeding Basilisks, Green Water Dragons, and Sail-tailed Dragons

To properly cycle these lizards, the photoperiod should be lessened during the winter months and the ambient temperatures reduced. Nine to ten hours of light will be sufficient. Night temperatures should range from the high 60s to very low 70s°F (18.9–22°C) and daylight temperatures should be only in the mid to high 70s°F (24–26°C). We suggest that you continue to provide a brilliantly illuminated basking spot with a surface temperature in the low 80s°F (27–29°C).

Nests

The lizards in this group usually dig well-formed nests in which to place their eggs, then cover the nests carefully following deposition. Because of this, it is necessary that they be provided suitable deposition areas. A mixture of sand, soil and peat, sufficiently deep—8 to 12 inches (20–30.5 cm)—and damp in consistency so that it will hold the shape of the nest that the female is digging, is required. The nesting medium can be provided in a deep plastic tub, a plastic terrarium, or even a large and deep plastic flowerpot. Pet green water dragons that have been given the run of a room have been known to jump into large low-hanging planters (suspended flowerpots) and deposit their egg clutch. Because basilisks are even more nimble than water dragons, they can be even more innovative in finding spots to seclude their clutches. Somehow, gravid female basilisks find their ways into what we would have thought to be insurmountable locations to lay their clutches.

Eggs

The eggs of these lizards are fairly large at deposition and increase noticeably in size as incubation progresses. Although the clutch sizes of some larger, older females have been known to number from 16 to 18 eggs, most clutches are much smaller. Clutches of water dragons and sail-tailed lizards usually number from 4 to 12 eggs. The most commonly reported clutch sizes for young females number between 5 and 9 eggs. Basilisks have smaller, and often more, eggs than the various dragons.

Temperatures for Incubating

Various breeders have suggested (and used) differing temperatures for incubating the eggs of basilisks, green water dragons, and sail-tailed lizards. These regimens vary from a constant of 84°F (28.9°C) throughout the entire 60 to 70 days of incubation, to a constant of 88°F (31°C) degrees. Other breeders suggest that the temperature be lowered somewhat, down from 87 or 88°F (30.6–31°C) to 84 or 85°F (28.9–29.4°C). We have learned that it is impossible to argue with success, but suggest that if you do use the 88°F (30.6°C) regimen, you do so only in a very sophisticated, commercial incubator. Be advised that 88°F (31°C) is very close to the upper lethal maximum for the eggs of many lizard species, and we feel that it gives no room, whatever, for even the slightest upward climb in temperature. Thermostats and incubators designed for such critical temperature control are much more expensive than any of the units we suggested earlier.

Hatchlings

The hatchlings of most of these lizards are hardy and easily reared.

Although most display decided insectivorous tendencies when babies, all should be offered vegetables and fruits as well as the typical insect fare. Some also enjoy lapping at a honey-fruit mixture (see page 38). Although some breeders recommend getting the hatchlings onto a diet of pinky mice as quickly as possible, it is our belief that a preponderance of mice is a very unnatural diet.

Hatchlings of some (the yellow-striped basilisk, for instance) are so small that fatal dehydration could occur quickly. They must be misted frequently, with a water receptacle available at all times, and provided with a high relative humidity in the cage.

Breeding Brown Water Dragons

Nearly everything said above for the green water dragon applies to this beautiful and interesting species as well. However, brown water dragons, being lizards of more temperate areas, seem to require a period of complete dormancy (brumation/hibernation) during the winter months. Without this, they usually fail to breed at all, and if eggs are produced, they are often inviable. For suggestions on properly hibernating this species, see pages 54–55.

About Anoles

Lizards that can change color have always been of interest to humans. Two groups known for this ability are the New World anoles and the Old World chameleons.

The anole family, Polychrotidae, has more than 275 described members, and probably many waiting to be discovered in tropical America. Overall, these are small-to-good-sized lizards, 6 to 18 inches (15–45.7 cm), some of which can change color from brown to green and back again. Males of all, and females of some, have distendable throat fans, which they use to signal other anoles (or humans, if you seem to be on their turf). The colors and patterns displayed on the throat fans are distinctive for each species.

The throat fans of anoles change appearance when viewed by reflected ultraviolet light, turning even the more blasé throat fans of some less colorful species into spectacular displays.

Anoles of several species are collected and sold as feeder lizards or as pets. The brown and the green anole are the species most commonly seen in both categories; however, the Jamaican giant, knight, and crested anoles are becoming more common in the pet trade. All of these types are rather easily kept, even bred, and are fairly long-lived. Longevity of wild-caught adults can range from four to eight years. Now that some species are being captive bred, longevity records of more than a decade can be expected.

Anoles Found in the United States

The Green Anole

The green anole, *Anolis carolinensis*, is native to the southeastern United States. It has been joined by several other species that, although not native, have been introduced and now are firmly established. This is a small lizard, with an adult size of about 6 to 7 inches (15–17.8 cm).

Range. The green anole has a natural range that includes virtually all of the Gulf Coast states, Georgia, the southern half of North Carolina, all of South Carolina, southeastern Tennessee, southeastern Oklahoma, and southern Arkansas. It has also been recorded in the Mexican state of Tamaulipas, and has become established in Japan.

Habitat. Green anoles are highly arboreal but occasionally may be seen on the ground. They have adapted well to most naturally occurring woodland conditions, being commonly seen

Except in southern Florida, where their dewlaps may be almost white, male green anoles have a pink dewlap.

Transverse lamellae on the toes of the anole gives purchase for climbing.

When cool, basking green anoles are brown, a color that quickly absorbs heat. When warm, if in the open the lizards are often a pale green; if in the shade they may remain brown. If active, green anoles are often just that, a bright green. If involved in aggression they are green but have a black patch behind each eye. A lighter

in cypress heads, among stands of oaks, in understories of rosemary and wax myrtle, in pine/palmetto scrublands, and even in certain tall native grasses. Populations of this lizard diminish as the land is developed. They are uncommon-to-absent in many urban and suburban settings.

Appearance. The color-changing abilities of the green anole are well known. An individual lizard may be brilliant green one minute and deep brown the next. The mechanisms that trigger these changes include stress, temperature, humidity, and light intensity.

As shown by this male green anole, most anoles are agile climbers.

Female green anoles often have a well-defined "zipper" of white middorsally.

When even moderately stressed, the green anole often assumes a brown coloration.

61

vertebral line is often present. This may appear zipper-like on females. Males are slightly larger than the females, and their tail base is heavier. The throat fan in the female is nonexistent to vestigial. Over most of the range, the male's throat fan is usually a pale pink. Some males in south Florida have white or pale cream throat fans.

Behavior. Male green anoles avidly defend their small territories against interlopers. The defended territory of each male is about 4 feet^3 (1.2 m^3) but the lizards routinely stray far beyond territorial boundaries. Males defend their perceived territory by compressing their body to appear larger, doing push-ups and head bobs and distending the throat fan. A low vertebral ridge may also be elevated. If this does not dissuade the interloper, the defending lizard will then sidle broadside toward the interloper, then dart toward and actually skirmish with the offender. The fights can be fierce, and will last until the interloper rushes off or the defender is deposed.

Anoles are habituated to human presence, and can turn our feeding devices to their own advantage. In one case, an anole has learned to drink sugar water from a hummingbird feeder.

Diet. Although the green anole is primarily an insectivorous species, individuals may also lap at nectar, pollen, or tree saps, the honey-fruit mixture (see page 38) and actually consume an occasional brightly colored flower petal or two.

Reproduction. As with all other anoles, the green anole is oviparous. From late spring throughout the summer, the female lays a single egg at fortnight intervals. Each incidence of ovarian development is stimulated by a courtship sequence. Since sperm can be stored in viable condition for periods exceeding eight months, actual copulation prior to each egg deposition is not essential. If a nest is prepared, it is a rather haphazard affair. A shallow scrape only slightly deeper than the diameter of the egg may be made in moist ground. As often as not, the egg is merely placed in leaf litter, amid trash heaps, or in similar moisture-retaining sites. Incubation averages two months. It may be somewhat less in hot weather, somewhat greater if climatic conditions are cool. Hatchlings are relatively large, often exceeding 2 inches (5.1 cm) in total length.

The Brown Anole

The brown anole, *A. sagrei* ssp., is now one of the most abundant lizard species in Florida. Other populations have been reported from Texas and in the New Orleans (Louisiana) area.

This anole, is not only an intergrade of two races, the Bahaman, *A. s. ordinatus*, and the Cuban, *A. s. sagrei*, but displays characteristics uniquely different from those of either parent race. Thus, we may surmise that we are seeing the firsthand development of a new subspecies.

Range. Because the brown anole is able to exist both in high population densities and in disturbed/modified landscapes, it has been incredibly successful in its spread throughout peninsular Florida. It may now be found south of a line drawn from Jacksonville to Lake City, then to Cedar Key. This spread is all the more amazing when you come to understand that the brown anole is quite cold-sensitive. At our home in Lee County (Ft. Myers) Florida, after a severe cold front—temperatures of 38°F (3.3°C) or below—dozens of dead *sagrei* could be found under shrubs. Obviously, enough survive cold fronts to repopulate and expand the lizard's range.

Habitat. The brown anole is less restricted to trees than any of our other anole species. It likes disturbed areas, and can be seen nodding and bobbing amidst grasses, on sidewalks, and from clearing edges, as well as from brush piles, heaps of building debris, or from low on the trunks of trees and shrubs. When frightened, rather than darting for the nearest tree, it darts into or beneath any available cover.

The brown anole is ostentatious in its territory defense, readily defending its territory against other anoles, dogs, birds, strange porch furniture, and humans. If you pause to bob your head at a male that is eyeing you quizzically, he will display his throat fan and bob back at you. This action will be repeated every time he sees you, just to make sure you understand who really belongs there.

Appearance. Typical of most anoles, male *sagrei* are much the larger of the two sexes both in length and proportionate heaviness of body. Males approach length of 8½ inches (21 cm). They are also the darker of the two sexes and usually lack all but traces of the dark-edged, scalloped, or straight middorsal stripe so typical of the juveniles and females. The throat fan of the males may vary from yellow-orange to orange and has a whitish border. When not distended, the border of the throat fan forms a light streak on the throat of the male lizard.

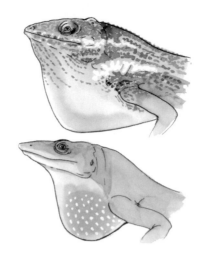

Size, facial markings and the shape of the dewlap help distinguish A. equestris *(above) from* Anolis carolinensis *(below).*

Some males have rather well-developed tail crests. Erectile nuchal crests are well developed and a vertebral crest slightly less so.

Diet. The brown anole likes small insects, including flies, crickets, small grasshoppers, nonnoxious caterpillars, mealworms, and small moths. They generally will not even taste mucous-laden feeder baits such as earthworms. They will lap at the honey-fruit mixture suggested on page 38.

Reproduction. Like the females of many other anoles species, those of the brown anole expend some effort in nest preparation. The single eggs are merely laid among plant debris, in a shallow scrape, on the ground beneath boards, cardboard, or other moisture-retaining material, and are produced at (about) 14-day intervals throughout the warm months. Eggs hatch in about 30 days. The hatchlings, feisty from day one, do not hesitate to make cursory territorial displays at any perceived threat.

Green versus brown. Certainly the green anole is less common than

Occasional male brown anoles are clad in scales of russet.

Now more commonly seen over much of Florida than the native green anole, the introduced brown anole, A. sagrei, is never green. This is an adult male.

before over large portions of its Floridian range. At one time it was thought that the intrusion of the brown anole was at least partly to blame, but since the two species prefer decidedly different ecological niches, it is more likely that it is the disturbed areas—the massive buildup in Florida—that is the cause. The brown anole is comfortable in these new habitats; the green is not.

Other pressures on the green anole also exist. The introduced knight anoles consume some of them. The pet industry uses this pretty little lizard by the thousands each year, and feral cats prey on them.

Three other color-changing anoles, the knight anole, *A. e. equestris*, the Jamaican giant anole, *A. garmani*, and the Hispaniolan green anole, *A. chlorocyanus* all are now established in Florida.

The Knight Anole

This Cuban native has been present in Florida for about three decades. Its presence is the result of a (or several) deliberate introduction(s).

Size. Not only is the knight anole the largest species found in Florida, it is the largest anole in the world. Adult males may slightly exceed 18 inches (45 cm) in length; the females are somewhat smaller.

Appearance. Although the knight anole is usually a brilliant green color, it is well capable of taking on a deep brown hue. In all colors, two light yellow-to-white flash marks are visible. The one on the shoulder is the most prominent, but the second, paralleling

At hatching, knight anoles are prominently banded and nearly as large as the adults of many other anole species.

the upper lip from eye to ear-opening will also be discernible. Widely spaced, contrastingly colored crossbars are also occasionally present. Interstitial (between scale) skin is colored differently than the scales. When visible this may create a reticulated pattern of contrasting colors. The rear of the knight anole's head is more heavily casqued, and its head proportionately larger than that of any other U.S. anole species. This is a truly impressive lizard species. The throat fans are present on both sexes. The fan of the male is of tremendous size, reaching from the anterior lower lip to well back on the chest. The fan of the female is proportionately smaller.

Behavior. Knight anoles are highly arboreal, usually keeping well up in the canopy during cool weather, but descending to the trunks below the canopy when temperatures are high. During mid-summer, knight anoles may descend to only a few feet above ground, where they often assume a head-down resting/hunting position on the tree trunks. Although knight anoles seem to prefer exotic foliage trees, we have also seen them on palms.

In comparison with other anole species, the knight anole is neither fast nor agile. In fact, it is rather easily approached if you move slowly. However, also unlike its congenerics, most of which rely on agility to avoid danger, knight anoles will stand their ground and can bite painfully hard. This fact has been attested to by many a collector.

Typically, before biting, a knight anole will present itself broadside to the source of its displeasure, laterally flatten its body, open its mouth, extend its immense dewlap (at least somewhat), and erect a prominent nape and anterior vertebral crest.

Diet. Knight anoles are omnivorous. Their large size allows them greater

This male brown anole has retained a complex middorsal stripe longer than most males do.

Male brown anoles are bulkier and darker than the females.

The dewlap of the male brown anole is brilliant and distinctive.

Female and juvenile brown anoles have a dark outlined, scalloped-edged vertebral pattern.

Appearance. The Jamaican giant anole is one of the color-changing anoles that is usually green but can darken to brown. Both sexes of the Jamaican giant anole have throat fans. That of the male is large, of a yellow coloration and may, or may not have an orangish center. The throat fan of the female is proportionately smaller and of a darker coloration. The pale dewlaps contrast strikingly with the usual bright green body color. Jamaican anoles have a low crest of enlarged serrate scales down their back and a more prominent nuchal (= nape) crest. Displaying males not only slowly distend, then retract the large throat fan, but through muscular contractions may elevate the vertebral crest more prominently as well.

latitude in prey items than that enjoyed by their congenerics. They eat insects, arthropods, other lizards, treefrogs, and fruit and berries. Larger examples of this large anole seem very fond of the fruit of the various Ficus (fig) trees and we have seen them consume the ripe berries of Virginia creeper.

Breeding. In our experience, a female temporarily kept captive deposited two eggs in the leaf litter at the bottom of her cage. Only one egg developed, the hatchling emerging after 67 days of incubation at ambient outdoor temperatures. It was quite dull in color. It is probable that like other anole species, female *equestris* deposit more than a single clutch annually during the late spring and summer months.

The Jamaican Giant Anole

This native of Jamaica is now well established in southern Florida.

Size. Although dwarfed by the knight anole, the Jamaican giant attains a far greater size than any of our other introduced anole species. Adult males often near a foot (30.5 cm) in overall length. The females are somewhat smaller.

Behavior. The Jamaican giant anole, like the knight anole, is rather more complacent about allowing close approach by humans than the smaller species. In the summer, the Jamaican giants that positioned themselves on the trunks of our shade trees would allow us to get within 2 feet (61 cm) of them. Any nearer than this and the lizards would tense, then dart away with a speed and agility unexpected from such a large creature. In this ability to effect an immediate response, they are very different from the much slower and larger knight anoles.

As with adult knight anoles, adults of the persistently arboreal Jamaican giant anoles divide their time between two niches. During the warmest weather *A. garmani* spends much time close to the ground on the trunks of large shade and palm trees. From that vantage point it hunts insects, typically while hanging in a head down position. Then it will not hesitate to leap to the ground to partake of a particularly succulent morsel. After grasping the prey, the lizard often returns to the tree to masticate and swallow.

Certainly capable of overcoming and consuming prey items as large as smaller lizards and treefrogs, *A. garmani* also seems to be less predaceous than *A. equestris*. We have frequently seen the much smaller brown anoles, *A. sagrei*, within inches of the jaws of *garmani* and have never witnessed predation.

Diet. *A. garmani* is omnivorous in feeding habits, avidly devouring crickets, grasshoppers, roaches, and other insects and arthropods. Some fruits, including the berries of the Virginia creeper vine, Ficus, and other vegetation are consumed. We once watched an adult male Jamaican giant anole high in a jacaranda tree lap up dozens, and perhaps hundreds, of small (unidentified) ants.

Range. Jamaican giant anoles were first collected from shade trees in Dade County, Florida about a decade ago. Although how they became introduced is speculative, it is thought that the original specimens escaped from pet dealers. Initially slow to expand, the species now seems rather well established both in Dade and Lee counties. We first noticed Jamaican giant anoles in Lee County, Florida, in 1988. By 1994 it was not uncommon to see five or six specimens on a warm summer afternoon.

Breeding. In Lee County, female Jamaican giant anoles deposit several clutches of one or two eggs during the hottest days of the year. We have seen the species breeding as early as April and as late as mid-September. Hatchlings have been found at various times from late July to early January. The hatchlings are often found amidst the greenery of ferns and on the slender upright stems of dracaenas and other garden plants. They are easily found at night sleeping on the broad leaves of syngonium, croton, philodendron, and other ornamental plants. The hatchlings and juveniles seldom display the brilliance of the larger *garmani*, often being pale green or pale brown and having vague spots and bars. By the time they are half-grown they have become more brilliantly colored, moved to intermediate and large-sized trees, and are much more difficult to find.

The Hispaniolan Green Anole

The most tenuously established of the color-changing anole species is *A. chlorocyanus*, the 9-inch-long (22.9 cm) (females smaller) Hispaniolan green. A Miami, Florida colony, known to have expanded over several city blocks, was apparently plowed into oblivion when the trees in which they dwelt were removed for construction, followed by a razing of the whole area. A second colony in Broward County, Florida was recently brought to my attention. During a visit to the area, we found the area overrun with the attractive brown-colored large-headed anole, *A. c. cybotes*, but saw only two females, two males, and a single juvenile *A. chlorocyanus*. All were high up in citrus, palm, and Australian pine trees and all were very shy, not allowing any type of close contact by us. As a matter of fact, they were so distant that even the photos taken with a 400mm lens left much to be desired.

Appearance. The Hispaniolan green anole is an attractive long-nosed creature that is quite reminiscent of our native green anole. However, rather than a pink, red, or white throat fan, such as is possessed by the native species, *chlorocyanus* has a cobalt blue dewlap. The dewlap is present on both sexes, but is much smaller on the female. Also, the tail scales of *chlorocyanus* are arranged in whorls of small and large scales, while the tail scales of our native species are all small. Adult male *chlorocyanus* average an inch or so larger than males of the native green anole.

Diet. Like many of the smaller anoles, the Hispaniolan green will eagerly lap at pollen, nectar, and the exudates from overripe fruit, but it appears that insects comprise the main part of the diet.

A. chlorocyanus was once imported in large numbers from Haiti by the pet trade. Escapees were able to continually bolster the numbers of feral specimens. Since importation has now become sporadic, it will be interesting to see whether this species continues to survive here.

Other Non-color-changing (Brown) Anoles of the United States

Of the remaining Floridian anoles, none ever assume a bright green color. In fact, three are predominantly brown and one is greenish gray.

Large-headed Anole

With a single small colony in Miami, Florida, and a second even smaller population in Hollywood, the large-headed anole, *A. c. cybotes*, has the most restricted range of Florida's brown-colored anoles. Despite its small size, the Miami population has existed in its circumscribed range since mid-February of 1967.

Although the adults of both sexes of the knight anole have dewlaps, the dewlap of the male (pictured here) is proportionately larger than that of the female.

Size. *Cybotes* is marginally the largest in body bulk of Florida's introduced brown-colored anoles (some male brown anoles, *A. sagrei* ssp. may near the bulk and slightly exceed the 8-inch (20 cm) length of male *cybotes* but male *sagrei* never develop the enlarged head of the latter).

Appearance. The vernacular name "large-headed" refers only to cranial size of the adult males of this Hispaniolan native. The heads of the females and the juveniles are of so-called "normal" proportions.

Large-heads are subtly but attractively colored. They are always of some shade of brown, occasionally with vague olive overtones. Often darkest dorsally, the flanks are, at times, notably lighter. Males have both a dorsolateral and a lateral stripe. Both are narrow and light (sometimes only vaguely visible), and they tend to converge posteriorly. The dorsolateral band is often broken into a series of spots. The contrast between dorsal and lateral colors seems the least when the animals are cool. A series of about a half-dozen dark crossbands may or may not be visible. If present, the crossbands may either terminate at, or be interrupted by, the contrastingly colored lateral stripe. The very large throat fan of the male, yellow to buff in coloration, may shade to pale orange centrally when distended. Males are capable of erecting vertebral and nuchal crests; the nuchal crest can be especially prominent. Female large-heads are very similar in appearance to the females of the ubiquitous brown anole, being brown to reddish-brown (lighter laterally), with a dark-edged light vertebral stripe. This stripe may be either straight or irregularly edged. Females also retain the light lateral stripes and often display one or two pairs of small, light shoulder spots, the anterior pair being the more discernible.

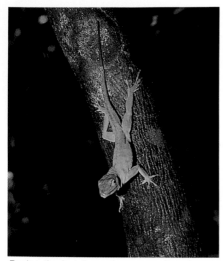

During the hot days of summer, Jamaican giant anoles thermoregulate, usually in a head down position, low on the trunks of shade trees.

Knight anoles have large heads, enlarged scales on the head, a yellowish mark from beneath the eye to the ear, and a low, erectable, crest of serrate scales on the nape.

Diet. Because of their large heads and correspondingly powerful jaws, male large-headed anoles are able to overpower larger prey than the females. They accept all types of suitably sized insects and arthropods. A male that we retained would also eagerly accept tiny terrestrial snails. Could the large head and powerful jaws have been developed for crushing the shells of such prey? Certainly a sexual difference in preferred prey items is far from unknown in the reptile world. As examples, the females of several of the map turtles (genus *Graptemys*) develop enlarged heads and the powerful jaw structure needed to crush the shells of bivalves, gastropods, and crustacea, the principal food items of adults. The males of the same species retain normally sized heads but do develop scissorlike mandibles, the better for dismembering the aquatic insects and small crustaceans of which their diets consist.

Although well able to climb, large-headed anoles are usually seen low on tree trunks, fences, building walls, and other such areas. After staking out their territories, adult males display while positioned head down on a prominent trunk or post, thus reinforcing territory boundaries. As the males display, the furling and unfurling of

The foot-long Jamaican giant anole, Anolis garmani, *is one of the most beautiful of all anoles. Males have a low serrate nape, vertebral and anterior tail crest.*

The Haitian green anole, A. chlorocyanus, *is present in a few discrete colonies in southern Florida.*

the pale but reflective dewlaps resembles the motions of a host of tiny semaphores.

Large-headed anoles are quick and agile when warm, then readily avoiding capture by most predators. However, they sleep in rather conspicuous places and are easily approached at night.

Breeding. The females that we have retained have deposited several clutches of one egg each at 14 to 20 day intervals throughout the warm months of spring and summer. Up to nine eggs have been deposited by individual females. Incubation duration has ranged from 31 to 46 days, depending upon temperature and humidity. Hatchlings are nearly 2 inches (5.1 cm) in length and resemble the females in color and pattern.

The Bark Anoles

The smallest of the anole species of the United States is the diminutive *A. distichus* ssp. Because of inconspicuous colors and patterns that blend remarkably well with the barks of the trees on which they are found, these 4½-inch-long (11 cm) lizards are commonly referred to as bark anoles (see photo page 72).

The bark anoles, of which there are at least five subspecies indigenous to the West Indies, are extremely quick and agile, hence adept at escaping predators once alerted. These little lizards sleep on broad leaves, then often assuming colors that contrast strongly with their background. At that time they are both easily found and approached.

Although bark anoles are often offered in the pet trade, they are not an easily kept species. The preferred diet of various ant species is difficult to replicate in captivity. We consider the several subspecies of this anole poor candidates for herpetoculture.

Appearance. Bark anoles are the smallest species of anole to become established so far in the United States. The pale yellow dewlap of the males and the dark dorsal chevrons of both species are distinguishing characteristics. Both color and pattern of these interesting little anoles are variable and provide the lizards with remarkable camouflage. Usually there is a series of dark chevrons (apices rearward) dorsally, a dark bar between the eyes, and a pair of light spots at the rear of the head. Although texts quote a green coloration for some races of this lizard, they are never as bright as the green anole. Seldom olive green, and most usually to some shade of tree bark gray or brown are the more usual colors. The tail and limbs of all races are prominently banded, this most conspicuous distally. The splay-legged scuttlings of this species are also somewhat different from the movements of other anoles.

Bark anoles are persistently arboreal and, although usually seen low on the trees, ascend rapidly if disturbed.

Florida range. The saga of the bark anole in Florida is somewhat complicated. Until rather recently there were at least three subspecies known to be represented here. These were *A. d.*

floridanus, the Florida bark anole (a gray or brown race with a pasty yellow throat fan) that was rather widely spread over much of Dade and Monroe counties, *A. d. dominicensis*, the "green" bark anole (a slightly greener race with an orangish dewlap) in Miami near the Tamiami Canal, and *A. d. biminiensis*, the Bimini bark anole (another pale race with an orangish-yellow dewlap), in Lake Worth. When initially discovered in Florida, the populations did not overlap; however, over the years, the populations of the two southern forms have grown and intermingled. As a result, *floridanus* and *dominicensis* cannot be differentiated.

In 1989 the bark anole was found in Lee County on Florida's southern Gulf Coast. Since then several adult specimens have been seen each year. No juveniles have yet been reported. Whether the Lee County population is sufficiently large to become viable, or will only exist for the lives of those individuals seen, remains to be seen.

Breeding. Female bark anoles produce successive clutches of a single egg each at two-week intervals from mid-spring to late summer. The eggs are placed among leaf litter with little or no attempt at nest construction. Incubation seems to take about 40 days.

The Crested Anole

Until recently the impressive crested anole, *A. c. cristatellus*, was known in Florida in only a few widely spread Dade County locations. These lizards have three crests, caudal (tail) crest, vertebral (body), and nuchal (nape) crests all being present. The nuchal and vertebral crests are voluntarily erectile through muscle contractions. The caudal crest, always at least vaguely discernible on adult males, is the one for which they are named.

With advancing age, males of the large-headed anole, A. c. cybotes, develop proportionately immense heads. The light lateral stripe is an identifying marking.

Appearance. *Cristatellus* is of Puerto Rican origin. A brown lizard, males have well-defined tail bands and may or may not have body blotches. The large throat fan of the male is pale yellow. Females look much like the more ubiquitous brown anole, having a dark-edged light vertebral stripe.

Like many other anoles, the crested stations itself rather low on tree trunks and fence posts, often in a head down

Except for the uninterrupted light lateral stripe, female large-headed anoles could be easily mistaken for females of other brown anole species.

position. From such vantage points, the males display and defend their territories against conspecific interlopers.

This is a fair-sized, robust anole of brown body color. The females are much smaller than the males. Males tend to have a higher crest on their tail than the male brown anole. The throat fan, or dewlap, of the male crested anole is light yellow to very pale orange, often with a darker border.

Male crested anoles, the only sex with the crest, attain a length of slightly more than 7 inches (17.8 cm). The females are much smaller.

Range. In recent years these lizards have spread widely and are now a frequently seen species in both urban and agricultural areas where they inhabit shrubs, brush piles, dumps, rock piles, and building walls and debris.

Diet. Primarily insectivorous, like most other anole species, crested anoles also lap nectar and pollen when it is available. Captives have enjoyed lapping the exudate of overripe fruit as well, such as a fruit-honey-water-vitamin supplement that we give most of our lizards (see page 38).

Rearward directed dark dorsal chevrons identify the bark anole.

Breeding. Although up to three eggs are reported per clutch, two captive females routinely deposited only a single egg at each laying. Each deposited an egg several times yearly in the leafy debris on the cage bottom.

The Sail-tailed Anole

A juvenile anole, of a species that at the time was not known to occur in Florida, was collected two years ago from high in a copse of shade trees in Lee County. We placed the creature in a cage in a large walk where it grew to a size that allowed identification. It was a male of *A. ferreus*, a large olive green to gray-blue species with a slate blue head and a high tail fin. The species is endemic to Marie Gallant Island in the West Indies.

Since finding the original specimen, we have returned to the area several times, once seeing two small anoles that we felt were referable to this species and, on a later trip, collecting three additional specimens of which there was no question of identification.

Size. *A. ferreus* is strongly dimorphic. The females seldom exceed 7.5 inches (19.1 cm) in overall length, but males often near 11 inches (28 cm). Females also lack the tail crest.

Diet. Since these are rather large anoles, they are able to consume a wider variety of invertebrates than smaller species.

Although it is too early to ascertain whether this species is actually established in southwest Florida, the fact that a minimum of four adult specimens have been found in the wild over a three-year period indicates that conditions are at least reasonably favorable. The true test will be when one of the rather rare freezes occurs in the area. We will be eagerly awaiting comments from future researchers.

About Larger Lizards

General Description

Because most of these lizards—basilisks and their relatives and water dragons and their relatives—are large, fast, and active, most will require disproportionately larger enclosures than members of the anole family.

The adults of the true basilisks and the water dragons all attain 2 feet (61 cm) or more in length, and should be maintained in terraria or caging of not less than 50 gallons (189 L) in size. Caging of at least twice this size (and preferably larger) would be far better.

The smaller basilisk relatives—the casque-headed and the cone-headed lizards—are smaller, naturally less active, and much less frenzied in their escape and avoidance responses than the true basilisks. Because of this, the casque-heads and the cone-heads may be maintained much like the anoles, in cages that are smaller proportionately to the overall size of the lizards.

To determine the preferred habitats of these lizards, consider their colors and body proportions—and envision a tree. For the basilisk family members—Corytophanidae—the green(ish), lightly built cone-headed lizards (*Laemanctus*) are the canopy dwellers. On the trunks, near the forest floor, are the brown cryptically-colored and shaped casque-headed lizards (*Corytophanes*). The heavy-bodied basilisks (*Basiliscus*) are found basking on horizontal branches at low to moderate heights, over quiet waters. This last area is shared by the water dragons (*Physignathus*) and sail-tailed dragons (*Hydrosaurus*) members of the family Agamidae.

The green basilisk of the New World and the green water dragon of the Old World are associated with overgrown, evergreen areas. While the brown basilisk and the brown water dragon may occur in forested areas, they are more typically creatures of open, deciduous scrub.

The basilisks, water dragons, and sail-tailed dragons are all typically associated with water courses or water holes and do not hesitate to enter water and submerge in efforts to evade predation. When frightened while on the ground, virtually all of the lizards in these genera (including the casque-headed and cone-headed lizards) run bipedally. Their hind legs are strong and can carry them quickly

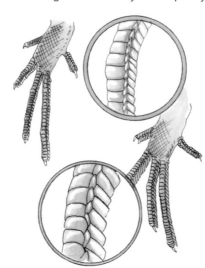

Both the basilisks and the sail-tailed dragons have flanges on their toes that aid in maneuvering on land and atop water, but the sail-tailed's (below) are much more pronounced.

from real or perceived threats, sometimes even across water.

Although the sail-tailed dragons, in most ways Old World ecological equivalents of the New World basilisks, have broadened toes, they have not yet shown an ability to run on water. Since they are fast, however, we would not be surprised if, under ideal conditions, they would be able to do so.

Diet. To the best of our knowledge, the two small members of the basilisk family—the cone-headed and casque-headed lizards—are predominantly insectivorous. However, it was not uncommon for us to find the cone-headed lizards eating heartily from the honey-fruit mixture (see page 38) containers positioned near the top of their cages. These pureed mixtures were provided basically for the cagemates of the cone-heads, the Malagasy day geckos, but were used extensively by the anoles as well.

The cone-heads would also nibble the petals from freshly picked hibiscus blossoms that we placed among the leaves in the top of their Ficus tree. We have not yet seen the little casque-headed lizards partake of

The spiny casque-headed iguanid, C. hernandezii *is not frequently seen in the pet trade. This was a very thin specimen.*

vegetable materials, but these lizards are so secretive that it would not be difficult to overlook them doing so. Certainly, if the casque-heads *were* to partake of the honey-fruit mixture, it would be from receptacles positioned lower in the cage (but probably not on the bottom) amidst the denser foliage.

The larger lizards—the true basilisks, water dragons, and sail-tailed dragons—eat insects of most kinds voraciously, but also readily feed on suitably sized mice (from "pinkies" to "jumpers," depending on the size of the lizards), canned dog foods, the honey-fruit mixture, blossoms, and some fresh fruits and vegetables.

The food insects included gut-loaded crickets and king mealworms, butterworms, waxworms, nonnoxious caterpillars, and June and other similar beetles. The fruits and vegetables included dark lettuces (leaf, romaine, escarole, etc.), some banana, apricots, peaches, grated apple, grated squash, dandelion greens and flowers, hibiscus leaves and flowers, nasturtium leaves and flowers, and many kinds of berries.

Water. This is important to all living creatures, and is garnered in many differing ways. Our cone-headed and casque-headed drank their fill of droplets immediately following a cage sprinkling. They are also most active during, or immediately following a light rainshower or a light misting from the hose. Heavy showers or heavy sprinklings will usually render the lizards inactive. The cone-heads will drink the individual droplets from the uppermost foliage, gingerly moving from drop to drop as if knowing instinctively that undue branch and leaf motion would cause many droplets to fall before they were reached by the lizards.

The casque-headed lizards, on the other hand, seemed to prefer to lick the water as it ran down the inner, vertical trunks of the Ficus, to which they usually clung. We found that correctly positioning one (or several) freshly filled drip bucket(s) above the tree would induce longer periods of drinking by the casque-heads than short mistings would.

Although the larger, partially aquatic, basilisks, water dragons, and sail-tailed dragons eagerly lap up the pendulous droplets left on foliage by rainshowers and mistings, they are less dependent on this method of drinking to retain suitable hydration than their smaller relatives. The three genera of larger lizards will readily drink from their containers of water. In the case of these larger lizards, the water container should be large enough for the lizard(s) to sit comfortably in. Because these lizards frequently defecate while in their water (indeed, entering the water seems to stimulate them to defecate), care must be taken that the water is changed as often as necessary. If several lizards are caged together, this can be often indeed.

In the wood-bottomed, outside cages that we used (and that can be used in most areas of the country during the summer months), keeping the water clean was a snap. The containers we use were the largest plastic kitty litter pans available. Fortunately, these have a prominent lip. With a small saber saw we cut a panel from the wooden cage bottom slightly smaller than the top of the water pan to be used. When properly cut, the pan can be inserted and will be suspended by its lip. We then drilled a hole for a large hard rubber stopper in the bottom of the water pan, stoppered it, and filled the pan with fresh water. The plug could be pulled as often as necessary, the container swabbed with a disinfectant, rinsed well, restoppered, and refilled. Each cleaning took only a few minutes. Although cleaning

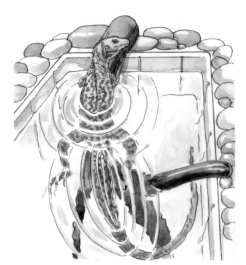

The water-loving sail-tailed dragon will soak if its water dish is large enough.

water is usually far more inconvenient in inside cages, we got around part of the problem by having a drain installed in the floor of our attached greenhouse. After this was done, we could easily dispose of the water once the pan was removed. Sterilizing, rinsing, and refilling also became easier when a small hose was used.

Remember: Dirty water is an ideal avenue for parasite transference between specimens. Keeping your lizard's water clean and fresh at all times is of paramount importance to the overall long-term health of any collection.

The Basilisks, Casque-headed, and Cone-headed Lizards

There are only 3 genera (9 species) in the family Corytophanidae. This breaks down to four species in the genus *Basiliscus*, the basilisks; three species of *Corytophanes*, the casque-headed lizards (often called "forest chameleons" or "helmeted iguanids"), and two species of cone-headed lizards of the genus *Laemanctus*.

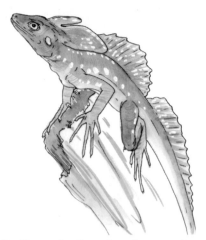

Basiliscus plumifrons is a showy creature, combining color, head casque, and vertebral and caudal crest.

All members of this family are oviparous (egg laying). All have some sort of head adornment. All are of Latin American distribution. All are lightly built with long limbs. All are agile climbers; in fact the Laemanctus are canopy species. Basilisks and

When you mist your lizard, point the sprayer upwards so the mist falls like rain.

cone-headed lizards bask frequently and often for long periods, especially during periods of cool weather or when relative humidity is low. Casque-headed lizards are less apt to bask, depending instead on suitably warm ambient temperatures being maintained at all times.

These lizards like high humidity. High relative humidity is maintained in the cage by providing a sizable, but shallow water dish as well as by periodic spraying (outside cages) or misting (inside cages). Growing plants also increase humidity in cages.

The Basilisks

The basilisks are veritable speedsters and excellent swimmers. When moving rapidly, they are bipedal. The large hind foot of the basilisk, in combination with long rear toes that bear a slight flange, provide a comparatively great surface area. Due to these specializations, the young (and to a lesser degree, some larger specimens) basilisks are capable of running across the surface film of quiet waters; however, if they slow, or stop, they sink. Within their natural Latin American range, the ability to "walk on water" gives rise to another common name for the basilisks, the "Jesus Christ" lizard.

Appearance. All four species within the genus Basiliscus have some degree of cranial cresting as well as gular pouches. Additionally, some basilisks have vertebral and/or caudal crests. The adornments are invariably better developed on males than females. The males of the basilisks are much longer and bulkier than the females.

Basilisks are frequently encountered resting quietly on the diagonal or horizontal branching of low shrubs that are in the proximity of water. Pond- and marsh-edge locations are favored. In Mexico, we have found *Basiliscus vittatus* very abundant in disturbed areas. On the occasions that we have stayed at hotels with nonenclosed swimming pools, the basilisks along the pool edge may considerably outnumber the often squeamish tourists.

When they are frightened, basilisks either dive into the water or rely on a headlong flight to escape. They are fast and wary.

Diet. The basilisks are insectivorous but will also add a nestling bird or baby rodent to their diet. In captivity some will also eat canned dog food. They may also nibble on blossoms and some fresh fruits and vegetables.

In captivity all will adapt to large well-planted terraria; outdoor step-in caging seems to be even better. Tropical daytime temperatures (85 to 95°F [29.5–35.0°C]) and high humidity are needed.

The Green Basilisk

The members of the genus *Basiliscus* are frequently seen in captivity, and of the four species of basilisks the hands-down favorite is the very beautiful green basilisk, *B. plumifrons*. Not only is this species the most brilliantly colored, but the males are the most prominently adorned of the four as well.

Adult males of the green basilisk have finlike crests on the back and tail and a double crest on the head. It is from the narrow, plumelike anterior cranial crest that the vernacular of *plumed basilisk* and specific name of *plumifrons* is derived.

The ground color is green (varying from light to dark), often with blue lateral spots and some vertical black markings in the vertebral crest. The iris is brilliant orange-yellow.

Adult males attain a length of more than 28 inches (71 cm). Adult females are several inches smaller.

We must reiterate that basilisks can be nervous lizards that if startled, may dash into the sides of the terrarium, sometimes resulting in severe nose

Green water dragons, Physignathus cocincinus, *of all ages often assume an alert, head up stance.*

(rostral) damage (see Nose Injuries, page 46). Wild-collected lizards tend to be more nervous than captive-bred and -hatched specimens. Strangely, males are often more nervous than females. It may be necessary to cover most of the glass of a basilisk terrarium with an opaque paper (or other such material) to prevent frightening the lizards.

The green basilisk is a species of forest pool, marsh, and swamp

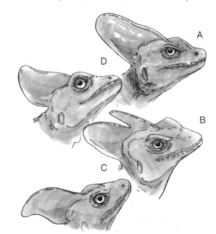

Basilisks can be differentiated by the size and shape of the head plumes.
A. Basiliscus vitattus, *B. B.* plumifrons,
C. B. galeritus, *and D. B.* basiliscus.

A pursued basilisk will run over water to evade capture.

edges. It ranges from Guatemala to Costa Rica.

Until recently, green basilisks have been only sporadically available to the pet trade. Currently, however, not only are large numbers of these lizards being collected and imported from Nicaragua, but captive breeding successes are now providing large numbers of hatchlings to hobbyists.

While less brightly colored than their green relatives, brown water dragons, Physignathus lesueuri, *are equally interesting.*

Foremost in the captive breeding of this species is Agama International of Montevallo, Alabama, a private breeding facility owned by Bert and Hester Langerwerf. More than 500 hatchlings are produced annually at this facility.

Dietary studies are still needed for with this species. Despite the fact that they live well and are rather easily bred, there is a noticeable tendency for captive-bred green basilisks to be duller—less intensely green—than those from the wild. Perhaps a higher concentration of beta-carotenes would reverse this trend.

Although it does not yet seem to be established, several green basilisks of both sexes have now been collected along Miami, Florida canals. All those we have seen looked like escaped or released wild-collected imports. All have had healed but still noticeable rostral injuries or other disfigurements that would have reduced their value in the pet trade.

The Two Brown Basilisks

B. basiliscus and *B. vittatus* are both a brown ground color. Both have wide yellow to white dorsolateral stripes and well-separated dark dorsal crossbars. *B. basiliscus* (Costa Rica to Colombia and Venezuela) has a well-developed (high) cranial as well as both vertebral and caudal crests. The adult males of both attain about 2 feet (61 cm) in overall length; the females are smaller. The head crest of *B. vittatus* is triangular, the vertebral crest is low, and the caudal crest represented by only a keel. This latter species occurs from Mexico southward to Costa Rica and is now firmly established along the canal systems of extreme southern Florida.

Although it is not as flamboyantly adorned as its more southern relative, *B. vittatus*, which we will call the northern brown basilisk, is a pretty and alert lizard. A horizontal shoulder stripe of the brightest yellow offsets the otherwise brown coloration nicely.

Although the specimens of this interesting lizard supplied to the pet trade of the United States are largely wild collected, they are no longer imported from Latin America in any great numbers. Rather, the pet industry specimens are now collected from canal-bank and canal-side vegetation in Dade County, Florida, where the species is now common and seemingly on the increase. Because of its ready availability to American hobbyists, the northern brown basilisk is seen in greater numbers in the American pet trade today than it ever was when the trade depended on imported specimens. Also, the domestically collected specimens now available are less stressed than the imports were.

Both the northern and southern brown basilisks have now been bred in captivity. Hundreds of hatchlings of the southern brown basilisk, *B. basiliscus*, are produced annually by Agama International. The owners, Bert and Hester Langerwerf, have found the species easily bred and the hatchlings hardy and comparatively easy to keep and size. As mentioned earlier, though, both species of brown basilisk can be nervous and easily startled. The immediate flight response of frightened specimens can (and usually does) result in nose injuries. The lizard is less inclined to dash away if it is approached very slowly and if the sides of its cage are opaque. Wild-collected animals are more nervous than captive-raised basilisks.

The Red-headed Basilisk

The coveted, but very infrequently seen red-headed basilisk, *B. galeritus*, of Ecuador and Colombia, has a well-developed cranial crest but the vertebral and caudal crests are represented by a series of enlarged flattened scales, each separated from the next by several small scales. The ground color of this pretty lizard is russet. Olive green highlights are present on the head and anterior trunk. Despite high prices, this lizard sells readily on the rare occasions when it is offered in the American pet market. Agama International is the only facility to have reported breeding this species.

The red-headed basilisk is a nervous and easily stressed lizard. If you are ever fortunate enough to acquire a pair, they will need a large cage with many visual barriers in an area of your house where foot traffic is minimal. Red-headed basilisks do not take well to even the most careful of handling. This is easily seen by the loss of color that occurs when the lizards are restrained. Bert and Hester Langerwerf of Agama International have found that even the hatchlings of the red-headed basilisk are more delicate and easily stressed than the babies of any other basilisk species. Unlike the babies of the green and brown basilisks, which can be easily raised in communal terraria, babies of the red-headed basilisk fare poorly when they are maintained in even small numbers. The Langerwerfs now raise each hatchling in an individual terrarium.

Casque-headed Lizards

There are three lizard species in this genus, but only one, *Corytophanes cristatus*, the common casque-headed lizard, is seen with any frequency.

In contrast to the rather smooth appearance of the common casque-head, the spiny casque-headed lizard, *Corytophanes hernandesi,* has isolated, elongate, spinous scales over the front portion of the upper body. The occipital ridges or crests are separate from the cranial crest.

The third species, *C. percarinatus*, is unknown in herpetoculture. It has keeled scales on the crown of the head and the occipital ridges do not

A male Basiliscus basiliscus *is an impressive sight.*

The Basiliscus vitattus *lacks a prominent vertebral crest.*

Basiliscus galeritus.

extend anteriorly much beyond the cranial crest.

Range. The common casque-head is found from southern Mexico to Colombia. The spiny casque-head is from Central Mexico to Guatemala, while *C. percarinatus* is from Oaxaca, Mexico, to El Salvador.

Appearance. Common casque-headed lizards are smooth-skinned, attractive creatures that are cryptically colored in earthen tones and that have variable light and/or dark bars. A distinct gular pouch is present. The occipital ridges are continual, with the canthi rising and nearly converging at the front of the very high and full cranial crest. A line of serrate scales, extending to the base of the tail, represents the vertebral crest.

Although an arboreally adapted forest species, these lizards prefer to remain in the understory. We have found them on the ground standing upon fallen leaves, on the horizontal trunks of fallen trees, and three feet or lower on the trunks of standing trees.

Behavior. *Corytophanes* has a curious method of escaping detection. At first, when startled, it may move away in a series of sporadic, froglike hops. Facing a predator such as a snake, it will turn its body broadside to the snake and flatten itself vertically, making itself look much larger than it actually is. If further frightened, it often becomes almost catatonic. It stiffens its body, tips its head downward, closes its eyes, and remains in that position for long periods. Once quiescent, the lizard virtually disappears against the fallen leaves of its woodland home.

Despite their quiet demeanor, casque-headed lizards do not enjoy being handled. When grasped, even gently, a specimen will stiffen and go into its catatonic-like state. If it becomes necessary to move or to otherwise handle a casque-head, let the lizard crawl up onto your hand. It will usually sit quietly on your hand or on a short section of suitably thick limb without physical restraint.

Corythophanes are difficult to acclimate, and should be considered delicate captives. They may be maintained in small groups of one male and one to three females, seemingly with no stress. Although ours are maintained for most of the year in sizable, heavily planted, walk-in cages, their quiet demeanor enables keepers to consider much smaller cages for these humidity loving lizards.

The shade-dwelling casque-headed lizards do not bask frequently. In their forestland homes, ambient temperatures are usually entirely suitable for optimum activity and body functions. In our Florida location, the walk-in cages were maintained outside and unheated at all times except during the passage of winter cold fronts. In the winter we affixed pliofilm to the outside of the cages as a windbreak. Heat was provided when nighttime temperatures dipped into, or below, the low 50s°F (10–12°C), but even during periods of comparative cold, our casque-heads seldom basked. A high humidity was always maintained

in the cages and during the hottest days of summer, the cage was sprayed several times daily or an overhead watering pail was utilized.

Size. Adult males may barely exceed 12 inches (30.5 cm) in total length, with females being marginally smaller.

Diet. These lizards are insectivorous, but the exact variety of their diet in the wild is at yet undetermined. They seem to be wait-and-ambush feeders, feeding on whatever insects stroll past them. Their diet in the wild may include ants. In captivity, feed dusted and gut-loaded crickets, and field plankton when possible.

Breeding. Casque-headed lizards are not currently captive bred in any great numbers. As a matter of fact, of the half dozen small clutches of eggs that our females have produced over the years, only three eggs, one in one clutch and two from another, were fertile. Since we had never seen the adults copulate, we were actually surprised that any eggs were fertile. The hatchlings were about 3.5 inches (8.9 cm) in total length. Of this, more than 50 percent was tail length. The cresting was poorly developed. The hatchlings did not survive. We know of no other captive breedings (and, indeed,

Of the basilisks, the green, Basiliscus plumifrons, is the species most sought by hobbyists. Note the intense green of this male (left) and female (right), both newly collected from the wild.

our meager success could have been due to sperm retention rather than on-site breeding).

Thus, with virtually no captive breeding known, the pet industry is entirely dependent on wild-collected imported specimens.

Cone-headed Lizards

The two species of cone-headed lizard, genus *Laemanctus*, bridge the gap between the speedy basilisks and the catatonic casque-headed lizards.

Of the two species of *Laemanctus*, it is usually *L. longipes* that is avail-able in the pet trade. This species, present from southern Mexico to Nicaragua, has a smooth posterior edge to the cone-like cranial casque. The cranial casque of the Mexican *L. serratus* is prominently serrate along its posterior rim.

Appearance and behavior. Although some researchers describe *Laemanctus* as being terrestrial, we have found them to be persistently arboreal. The cone-heads are alert predators of canopy insects. There, their greens and tans render the lizards virtually indiscernible. The cone-heads lack vertebral or caudal

This very blue male green basilisk was photographed at the National Serpentarium in San Jose, Costa Rica.

Of the brown basilisks, the prominently crested males of the southern brown basilisk, B. basiliscus *are the most eagerly sought by hobbyists.*

The ventral scales of female B. basiliscus (pictured) lack keels; those of the lookalike B. vittatus *have keels.*

With age, the pattern of the male northern brown basilisk, B. vittatus, *dulls and the head-crest attenuates.*

cresting, having only the flat-topped ridge at the back of their heads as adornment. This is equally developed in both sexes.

Both species of these lizards have tails three or more times the combined length of their head and body. Adults measure up to 18 inches (45.7 cm) overall. Hatchlings measure about 7 inches (17.8 cm) in total length, of which all but 1.75 inches (4.5 cm) is tail.

Specimens in our walk-in cages spent most of their time in the crowns of the small Ficus trees that grew in the 6-foot-tall (183 cm) enclosures.

Cone-heads are usually quite inactive but are capable of bursts of considerable speed. When pressed, they are able to jump rather nimbly from leafy branch to leafy branch in escape efforts. Their long hind legs give them a somewhat ungainly appearance, belying the actual agility of the lizards.

Diet. Our lizards eagerly accepted vitamin-dusted crickets that climbed to their "canopy" home and would even more eagerly leap in acrobatic attempt to snatch flying moths from the air. Even within the constraints of the cage, the lizards seldom missed.

Besides the characteristic red head, adult males of the Ecuadorian B. galeritus *have a greenish body and lack both body and tail crests.*

Clad in dead-leaf browns, the common casque-headed "iguanid," Corytophanes cristatus, *is an attractive but delicate captive.*

A penny lends perspective to the size of a several-day-old northern brown basilisk.

Laemanctus longipes, *the smooth cone-headed iguanid, is now rather frequently seen in captivity.*

Green water dragons are being bred in captivity with increasing frequency. These two are several weeks old.

Hatchlings fed more reluctantly, needing tiny feed insects and absolute quiet before they would accept their first few meals. Hatchlings are very prone to dehydration, but once they begin feeding they are no more delicate than the hatchlings of most lizards.

The cone-heads of all sizes, but especially the hatchlings, are reluctant to drink water from a dish, even when the water is stirred by an aquarium air stone. However, all of the lizards drink water droplets from the foliage when

Although of similar coloration, male green water dragons (right) have larger crests than females.

the cage is sprayed or misted or, outside, during periods of natural rainfall.

Breeding. Several hobbyists and zoos have bred these lizards. The females multi-clutch each year, laying one to three eggs per deposition.

Although both species of cone-headed lizards have a reputation for being delicate, it is primarily dehydration the makes them so. Internal parasites are often a secondary problem. In concert the two problems can quickly be devastating. If newly acquired *Laemanctus* are promptly rehydrated, then treated for endoparasites, they will often live for years.

Water Dragons and Sail-tailed Dragons

The water dragons, *Physignathus,* and the closely allied sail-tailed dragons of the genus *Hydrosaurus,* are beautiful and, if properly stabilized, hardy lizards of moderate size. Usually considered less nervous than basilisks, the difference can be marginal where wild-collected adult specimens are involved. And, if a degree of nervousness can be assigned, we would have to say that the sail-tailed lizards are usually more flighty than the water dragons.

When newly collected, wild-caught specimens of either water or sail-tailed dragons are received, unless great care is taken to prevent it, they will soon have their noses bruised and bloodied from continued escape attempts. Sometimes this will happen no matter what precautions are taken, but in general, secure, stress-free quarters will help you attain initial success with all of these lizards.

In all cases, whenever it is possible, we suggest that you begin your relationship with these lizards by acquiring captive-hatched specimens. If these are *not* available, hold out for immature wild-collected specimens. You will have better success taming, or at least quieting, a young specimen than an adult. In fact, wild-collected adult specimens of the various sail-tailed dragons may *never* become tame, no matter how much effort you expend, and taming some wild-collected adult water dragons may prove only slightly less difficult.

Water Dragons

Unlike the anoles, basilisks, and their relatives, which are of exclusively New World distribution, the two species of water dragons, genus *Physignathus* are just as exclusively Old World. They are members of a huge family, the Agamidae. Actually, although two species are currently contained in the genus, it is likely that one, the Australian brown water dragon, will soon be reclassified. Researcher Scott Moody has found that the brown water dragon is more closely allied to the sail-tailed dragons of the genus *Hydrosaurus* than to its green relative. It seems probable that a new genus will be created for the brown water dragon.

The Green Water Dragon

Water dragons are hardy, magnificent lizards of moderate size. Both are now being extensively bred in captivity, but wild-collected specimens of the southeast Asian green water dragon, *P. cocincinus*, continue to be imported to both America and Europe in large numbers. Prices for the green water dragon reflect this ready availability of wild specimens, deflating the prices of even captive-bred specimens. Adult imported green water dragons may sell today for as little as $25, captive-bred hatchlings might be a little more. On the other hand, the brown water dragons, an endemic Australian species, are protected and not currently imported by the pet trade in any great numbers. Although less colorful than the green, the relative rarity of the

Although sexes are difficult to differentiate until the lizards are adult, the diagonal side striping of even young male green water dragons is often a bright blue.

brown water dragon insures that they seldom sell for less than $150 each. Again, captive-bred and -hatched brown water dragons are usually somewhat more expensive than the few imported specimens.

The two species of water dragon are easily differentiated. As indicated by its name, the Southeast Asian *P. cocincinus* is of some shade of green

Unless handled almost daily from the time they hatch, male brown water dragons can be difficult to approach. A photographic blind was utilized for this photo at Agama International.

85

This is a subadult female brown water dragon.

dorsally. The actual shade of green may vary somewhat by population (lizards from one circumscribed area may not be the same shade as those from a distant area) and the color *certainly* varies according to degree of stress (or lack of stress) being felt by the lizard. Stress, as used here, may indicate one or a combination of factors, including, but not necessarily limited to, adverse temperatures, physical restraint, endoparasitism, territorial encroachments by other lizards, or fright. Dominant, sexually active male green water dragons often display the brightest green of all, and may have a yellow or peach suffusion on the throat and anterioventrally. A well-defined vertebral crest extends from nape to about half way down the lizard's tail. Body bands, when present, are light; tail bands (almost always prominent, especially on the distal two-thirds of the tail) are dark. When dominant males are indulging in territorial displays, the nuchal crest is prominently raised.

With a distribution over much of southeast Asia, green water dragons are more exclusively tropical, hence more cold-sensitive than their brown cousins. Most of the specimens currently (1996) being imported are from Vietnam. These specimens seem to be somewhat darker in coloration as well as a little smaller then those that used to be imported from Thailand.

The Brown Water Dragon

The second species, *P. lesueuri*, is called either the Australian or the brown water dragon. It, too, is aptly named. It is gray-brown to brown and darkest dorsally, caudally, and on the limbs. Light bands are present on the body and tail; light flecks are present on the limbs. Mature specimens have a suffusion of dark red ventrally. This is brighter on the male than the female, and brightest on sexually active males. Except on the nape where it is represented by a few rather tall scales, the vertebral crest of the brown water dragon is vestigial. Dorsal and lateral scalation is markedly heterogeneous (includes scales of many varying sizes).

The babies of both water dragons are lighter in color than adults and mature males of both develop a jowly look.

Of the two species of water dragon, the brown is the larger. Occasional males may near 3 feet (0.9 m) in total length. Most are smaller and females are always smaller. Males of the green water dragon occasionally attain 30 inches (76 cm) in total length. The tail of both species accounts for slightly less than two-thirds the total length.

If obtained while young, water dragons tame well and usually remain quiet and easily handled as they mature. Although wild-collected adults live well, they often resent familiarity and frequently injure their noses in attempts to escape. They are seldom as flighty as wild-collected basilisks, however.

It would appear that water dragons are primarily insectivorous in the wild but may consume an occasional small vertebrate and a little fruit and a few flowers as well. In captivity they readily accept small mice, canned cat food, insects, and some fruits, flowers, and vegetables. Both species are oviparous. Females dig deep nests in which they deposit from 8 to 14 eggs. At 86°F (30°C) the eggs hatch in from 72 to 90 days.

Note: The hatchlings of both species are very hardy and, if adequately nourished, grow quickly. However, females may not produce viable eggs until their third (or even their fourth) year of life.

Ecologically, water dragons seem to fill much the same niche as green iguanas. Water dragons are most commonly encountered near water while basking on elevated perches. They often choose perches that enable them to drop directly into the water when startled.

In captivity water dragons prefer sizable cages with a large water receptacle. Mine have done best in walk-in cages in which potted Ficus trees provide visual barriers and horizontal limbs at numerous elevations offer ample resting perches. Large containers of clean water are kept in the cages. The dragons often sit or even submerge in these, at times for long periods. Dragons often defecate in their water receptacle, so the water must be changed and the containers scrubbed frequently.

Sail-tailed Dragons

What's a sail-tailed dragon? Since some basilisks truly are "sail-finned" lizards, having prominently raised fins on head, trunk and tail, and since the members of the genus *Hydrosaurus* have a fin only on their tails, we have always felt the name "sail-tailed" more descriptive than the often seen name of sail-finned dragon. As far as the "dragon" part goes, many Old World lizards are colloquially known as dragons, and since these lizards are quite closely allied to the Old World water dragons (which are known almost everywhere as "dragons"), the common name of sail-tailed dragon seems rather quite appropriate.

The sail-tailed dragon has a crest along its backbone and a pronounced fin or sail along its tail.

The sail-tailed dragons are fairly large in size. As with many lizard species, adult males can be up to 35 percent larger than adult females.

The sail-tails form a genus of two or three species of magnificent agamids: One, the Amboina sail-tailed dragon, *H. amboinensis*, is marginally the world's largest agamid. Adult males of this species push may slightly exceed 4' (120.8 cm) in length, a measurement most closely approached by some male frilled lizards. Although smaller, the remaining two species of sail-tails, the Philippine, *H. pustulatus*, and the Indonesian, *H. weberi*, also attain impressive sizes.

In private and public collections in the United States, neither the Philippine nor the Indonesian sail-tailed dragons are uncommon. The Amboina dragon is rare.

It is as babies-to-half-grown size that the various hydrosaurs are usually available. As baby-to-small-juveniles, the Philippine species is very inexpensive. Fewer of the Indonesian species are imported, hence those available command a higher price.

As babies, none of the hydrosaurs have the adornment for which they are named. In fact, the sail is still vestigial on half-grown specimens and remains

Male Weber's water dragons, Hydrosaurus weberi, *(above) are larger and more brilliantly colored than the females (below).*

Sail-tailed dragons have broadly flanged toes, suitable for running in marshy and muddy areas, and perhaps even across the surface of still waters. Pictured is a young Philippine sail-tailed dragon, Hydrosaurus pustulatus.

quite low on adult females. It is the adult males that lend credence to the common name of sail-tailed dragon. On the males, the sail rises above the "body of the tail" for at least the diameter of the tail.

None of the sail-tailed dragons are colorful lizards. Babies of the Philippine species are olive tan laterally, often somewhat darker middorsally and with light vertical bars along the side. The adults are darker. Old males can be an unrelieved olive brown.

H. weberi is somewhat dichromatic. Females tend to be olive to olive brown with darker and lighter barring laterally. Males are olive green (lightest anteriorly) with dark barring. *H. weberi* also darkens with advancing age. We have not seen the juveniles of *H. amboinensis*, but the adults we have seen have varied from a boldly reticulated black on olive to a nearly unrelieved olive brown. The females were somewhat lighter than the males.

Like many of the big active agamas and iguanids, wild-collected adult hydrosaurs are nervous, hence often unsatisfactory captives. They seem unable to adjust to confinement in a cage. If approached (even slowly!) they may dart repeatedly into the sides of their enclosure, injuring their snouts and jaws in the process. This injury results in a reluctance to feed, which leads to the animal's death. On the other hand, babies are relatively quiet and remain that way as they grow.

Hydrosaurs are oviparous. Adult females lay from 4 to 18 eggs. Despite being coveted lizards, few persons or institutions are currently breeding either species. Eggs should be incubated as for the green water dragon, at between 82 and 86°F (28–30°C).

Sail-tailed lizards are quite omnivorous. Besides insects and suitably sized rodents, these lizards will quite readily accept many vegetables and sweet fruits at all stages of their lives.

Photographing Your Lizards

For many lizard-keepers, photographing the animals we keep is just a logical extension of caring for these lizards and studying them. It is a good way to document captive or wild behavior patterns. Good slides are certainly excellent educational tools and can be used as "museum vouchers" to officially document the existence or behavior of the animal in question.

Capturing a lizard—big or small—on film often requires a great deal of patience and discipline. You either quickly learn from your mistakes, or they become quite costly. Each photo helps you to see how the next could be improved.

The equipment you will need depends upon a number of variables. Among these are whether you will be indulging in both long-distance field photos (sometimes necessary for many canopy species) and staged closeups. Of course, photographing captive or staged lizards is infinitely easier than pursuing and photographing free-ranging ones. Although some photographers feel it is not nearly as satisfying, it is also the only way you'll ever get a closeup of some of these species.

Some Photographic Hints

Staged photography. Create a small natural setting by placing leafy branches or bare limbs appropriate for the species you're photographing—on a stage. Our stage consists of a small, well-doctored and augmented lazy Susan. When we chose it as a stage,

it was with the thought that we could rotate the stage with the animal on it, for different photographic angles. It was a good thought, and it actually works, providing that you move very slowly, both in your own actions and in rotating the stage. If you don't have a lazy Susan, just arrange the setting items on a tabletop or on a tree stump (outdoors or in, depending on where you are at the time), put the lizard in place, focus, and shoot. Having a photo assistant to help pose or catch the (escaping) lizard, whichever is applicable, will help.

The stage. We created a portable stage with a heavy-duty round plastic trash can, inverted and cut to size, then firmly bolted into place atop the lazy Susan base. Black velvet clipped into place around the inside surface of the trash can gives a good, nonreflective, background for the lizard shots.

A 35 mm camera body and several lenses will enable you to capture lizard(s) on film.

Basic Equipment

A sturdy 35 mm camera body with interchangeable lenses is suggested. Many of the newer cameras claim to be point-and-shoot cameras, and to a great extent this is true. We have not yet seen a single camera with attached lens and built-in strobe that can do everything, from closeups to wide angle to telephoto shots.

You don't necessarily need a brand-new camera body and lenses; we've used quality secondhand equipment for many photographic ventures. You do need a photo supply dealer who can advise you about the condition of the equipment you're buying, and who can tell you about some features of that particular lens or body (usually speaking, secondhand camera equipment does not come with manuals of any sort).

Lenses. The lenses we use include:

28 mm wide angle for habitat photos

50 mm standard for habitat photos

100 mm macro for closeups (suitable for almost every purpose)

75–205 mm zoom lens for variable field work

400 mm fixed focal length telephoto lens for field work

120–600 zoom lens for distant but variable field work

Strobes. A series of dedicated strobes (a dedicated strobe interfaces with the camera f-stop setting to automatically furnish appropriate light levels).

Lens adapter. An ×1.25 power magnifier or an ×2 doubler.

Film. ISO 50-slide film is slower and less "grainy" than higher speed films. This slower film will give you the best results, but also requires a bright day or electronic flashes to compensate for the slow speed. The higher the ISO of the film, the less light you will need to photograph, but the grainier your pictures will be. If you are taking pictures with the hopes of having them published, use ISO 50-slide film and adapt your methods to its requirements. If you are taking photos merely for your own enjoyment, use either slide or print film, as you prefer.

Tripod. A sturdy tripod (an absolute necessity for the telephoto lenses) will hold your camera steady while you squeeze off that "once in a lifetime" shot of a Jamaican giant anole high in an unscalable tree. Camera equipment-with-lenses is heavy. You'll find it heavy even indoors. And, after a day in the field, when you are tiredly slogging your way back toward where you think you've parked your vehicle, the weight of your equipment seems to grow exponentially with each increasingly weary step. There may be times when you will want to carefully consider exactly what equipment will be required. Then, after paring things to the bare minimum, if you're really adept at field photography, you will succeed in talking your companion into carrying the equipment for you. Of course, when you're five miles from the car, you'll often find that you could have gotten the world's best photo of _____ (you fill in the blank), if only you had brought a different lens!

Camera body. After having a camera body malfunction on occasion, we now always have at least one spare body available. This is especially important if you are photographing in the field.

The end result has been an easily moved, eminently serviceable stage.

Field photography can be considerably more trying than staged photography. To successfully accomplish the former, it is almost mandatory that you have an assistant. An assistant helps carry the equipment, change film, spot the animal, keep an eye out for other animals while you're photographing the first, and position a hand-held strobe. We generally try to first make field photos, then capture the specimen temporarily, and take staged photos. Between the two approaches we often get excellent results.

Finding the subject(s). Fortunately, the lizards covered in this book are diurnal lizards. This enables you to dispense with the flashlights and other paraphernalia needed to successfully photograph nocturnal species. Generally, if you move very slowly and avoid making eye contact, anoles will

A stage will enable you to pose your lizard for photography.

remain in place long enough to permit you to get a few shots. Basilisks and the other larger lizards may be more wary and will take more caution.

Useful Addresses and Literature

Bibliography

Demeter, Bela J., "Captive Maintenance and Breeding of the Chinese Water Dragon, *Physignathus cocincinus*, at the National Zoological Park." *Proceedings of the 5th Annual Reptile Symposium on Captive Propagation and Husbandry* Thurmont, MD (1981).

Mader, Douglas R., "Chinese Water Dragons, *Physignathus cocincinus.*" *Reptiles Magazine*, (1994) 2:1

Mitchell, Lyndon A., "Comments on the Maintenance and Reproduction of *Hydrosaurus pustulatus* at the Dallas Zoo." *Proceedings of the 9th International Herpetological Symposium on Captive Propagation and Husbandry* Thurmont, MD (1985).

Information and Periodicals

Lizard species that once were rare in the private sector are increasingly available from both private and commercial breeders and importers.

Many sources advertise in the various reptile and amphibian magazines, some of which are listed below:

Reptiles
P.O. Box 6050
Mission Viejo, CA 92690

Reptile and Amphibian Magazine
RD 3, Box 3709-A
Pottsville, PA 17901

Reptilian
22 Firs Close Hazlemere
High Wycombe, Buck HP15 7HF
England

The Vivarium (the publication of the American Federation of Herpetoculturists)
P.O. Box 300067
Escondido, CA 92030

Herpetological Ecotourism

Green Tracks, Inc.
P.O. Box 9516
Berkeley, CA 94709
Telephone: 800-966-6539 (USA) or 510-526-1339 (worldwide)

Affinity Groups

Herpetological/herpetocultural clubs can be found in many large cities. Check with the biology department of your nearest university, or with the personnel of nature centers or museums to find the club nearest you.

Glossary

Aestivation A period of warm weather inactivity; often triggered by excessive heat or drought.

Agonistic Antagonistic, hostile.

Allopatric Not occurring together but often adjacent.

Ambient temperature The temperature of the surrounding environment.

Anterior Toward the front.

Anus The external opening of the cloaca; the vent.

Arboreal Tree-dwelling.

Autotomize The ability to break easily, or to voluntarily cast off (and usually to regenerate) a part of the body, such as the tail.

Bipedally As used here, running on the two hind legs.

Brumation The reptilian and amphibian equivalent of mammalian hibernation.

Caudal Pertaining to the tail.

cb/cb Captive-bred, captive-born.

cb/ch Captive-bred, captive-hatched.

Chitin The material of which the hard exoskeleton of insects is composed.

Cloaca The common chamber into which digestive, urinary, and reproductive systems empty and that itself opens exteriorly through the vent or anus.

Convergent evolution Evolution of two unrelated species as the result of environmental conditions.

Crepuscular Active at dusk and/or dawn.

Deposition As used here, the laying of the eggs.

Deposition site The spot chosen by the female to lay her eggs or have young.

Dewlap (also called throat or gular fan) A voluntarily distendable fan of skin on the throats of anoles; these are either missing or comparatively small on females.

Dimorphic A difference in form, build, or coloration involving the same species; often sex-linked.

Diurnal Active in the daytime.

Dorsal Pertaining to the back; upper surface.

Dorsolateral Pertaining to the upper sides.

Dorsum The upper surface.

Ecological niche The precise habitat utilized by a species.

Ectothermic Cold-blooded.

Endothermic Warm-blooded.

Form An identifiable species or subspecies.

Genus A taxonomic classification of a group of species having similar characteristics. The genus falls between the next higher designation of "family" and the next lower designation of "species." Genera is the singular of genus. It is always capitalized when written.

Gravid The reptilian equivalent of mammalian pregnancy.

Gular Pertaining to the throat.

Heliothermic Pertaining to a species that basks in the sun to thermoregulate.

Hemipenes The dual copulatory organs of male lizards and snakes.

Hemipenis The singular form of hemipenes.

Herpetoculture The captive breeding of reptiles and amphibians.

Herpetoculturist One who indulges in herpetoculture.

Herpetologist One who indulges in herpetology.

Herpetology The study (often scientifically oriented) of reptiles and amphibians.

After being fed a diet of commercially raised insects, many green basilisks become more blue than green. Beta-carotene additives may prevent or even reverse this.

Hydrate To restore body moisture by drinking or absorption.

Juvenile A young or immature specimen.

Labial Pertaining to the lips.

Lateral Pertaining to the side.

Middorsal Pertaining to the middle of the back.

Midventral Pertaining to the center of the belly or abdomen.

Nuchal crest A crest, often voluntarily erectile, on the nape of the neck.

Oviparous Reproducing by means of eggs that hatch after laying.

Photoperiod The daily/seasonally variable length of the hours of daylight.

Poikilothermic A species with no internal body temperature regulation.

Race A subspecies.

Rostral The (often modified) scale on the tip of the snout.

Setae The microscopic hairlike bristles in the subdigital lamallae of an anole's toes.

Species A group of similar creatures that produce viable young when breeding. The taxonomic designation that falls beneath genus and above subspecies. Abbreviation: "sp."

Subdigital lamellae The transverse plates (groves and ridges) that extend across the undersurface of an anole's toes.

Subspecies The subdivision of a species; a race that may differ slightly in color, size, scalation, or other criteria. Abbreviation: "ssp."

Sympatric Occurring together.

Taxonomy The science of classification of plants and animals.

Terrestrial Land-dwelling.

Thermoreceptive Sensitive to heat.

Thermoregulate To regulate (body) temperature by choosing a warmer or cooler environment.

Thigmothermic Regulating body temperature by basking on or beneath a sun- or otherwise warmed object.

Vent The external opening of the cloaca; the anus.

Venter The underside of a creature; the belly.

Ventral Pertaining to the undersurface or belly.

Ventrolateral Pertaining to the sides of the venter (=belly).

Vertebral crest (also, middorsal crest) The raised scales, either single or fused, along the middle of the lizard's back.

Index

*Somewhat bulkier than the very similar brown anole,
crested anoles may or may not have a prominent tail
crest. Male crested anoles have a pale-yellow dewlap.*